PICTURES OF THE YEAR
Annual Photo Competition and Exhibition

The University of Missouri School of Journalism and the
National Press Photographers Association are pleased to
announce that the Pictures of the Year competition is
now being supported by Canon U.S.A., Inc. through an
educational grant.

Ken Kobre, University of Missouri
Pictures of the Year Contest Director

With admiration and respect, this book is dedicated to Joseph Costa, a news photographer, teacher, editor and leader, who in his 80th year is still giving full measure — sifted, pressed down, and overflowing — to the profession he loves.

*An annual based on the 41st Pictures of the Year competition
sponsored by the National Press Photographers Association and the
University of Missouri School of Journalism*

2

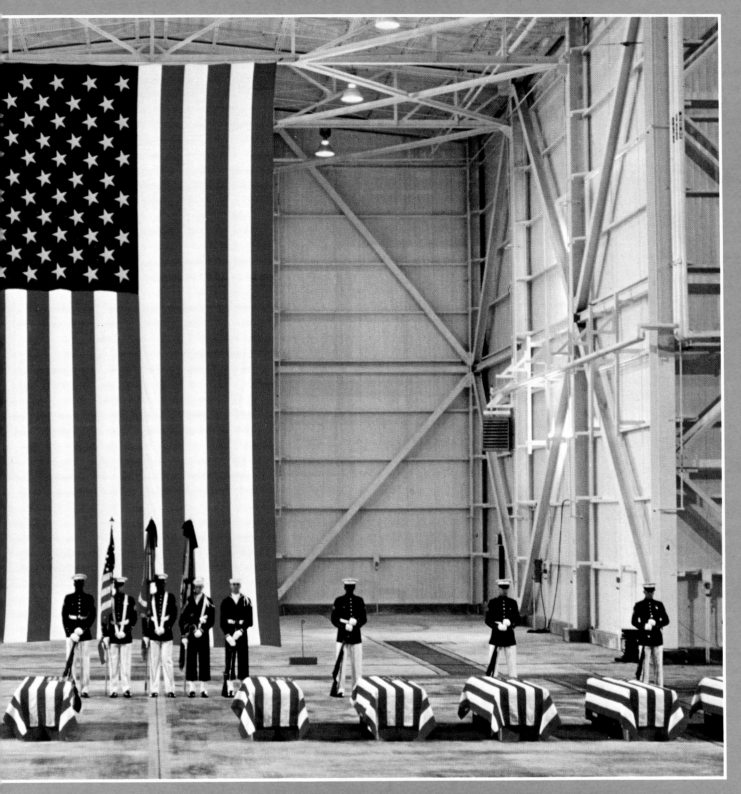

The best of
Photojournalism/9

RUNNER-UP, NEWSPAPER PHOTOGRAPHER OF THE YEAR, MICHAEL BRYANT, SAN JOSE (CALIF.) MERCURY NEW

PRECEDING PAGE: U.S. Marine casualties from Beirut and Grenada. Photo by Mark Meyer for Time.

Above, bus driver Art Schmeister decided the correct attire for the inauguration of California Gov. George Deukmejian was a cap and Old Glory.

FRONT COVER: Just another normal load for Raymond Baez, who hand-trucks merchandise a block and a half in downtown Hartford, Conn. (See Page 126.) The photo is by Paul Miller, freelance for The Hartford Courant.

REAR COVER: Portrait of 84-year-old nursing home resident cuddling a baby chick won first place in the newspaper portrait/personality division of the 41st annual Pictures of the Year competition. Photographer is Jimi Lott, Spokane (Wash.) Review and Chronicle. (See Page 82.)

Cal Olson, editor
Joanne Olson, assistant

Copyright © 1984
National Press Photographers
Association, Box 1146
Durham, N.C. 27702

Library of Congress Catalog
Number: 77-81586

ISBN: 0-89471-247-0
(Paperback)
ISBN: 0-89471-248-9 (Library
binding)

ISSN: 0161-4762

Printed and bound in the
United States of America by
Jostens Printing and Publishing
Division, Topeka, Kansas
66609.

Contents

Distributed by Running Press Book Publishers, Philadelphia, Pennsylvania. Canadian representatives, General Publishing, 30 Lesmill Road, Don Mills, Ontario M3B 2T6. International representatives: Kaiman & Polon, Inc., 2175 Lemoine Avenue, Fort Lee, New Jersey 07024.

This book may be ordered by mail from Running Press Book Publishers, 125 South 22nd Street, Philadelphia, Pennsylvania 19103. Please include $1.50 for postage and handling. But try your bookstore first.

For information concerning the Pictures of the Year Competition, contact Charles Cooper, NPPA Executive Secretary, Box 1146, Durham, North Carolina 27702. Cover design by Running Press.

In Paris, flag-draped caskets of Frenchmen killed in the Beirut bombing are laid in lines at a memorial ceremony at Las Invalides.

Anno Domini 1983:
Flags and funerals

1983 will go down as a year of flags and funerals — flags draped over the caskets of those who died in war and of those who died in blind, terroristic incidents.

The agony of military conflict came home to the United States during the Marines' peacekeeping mission in Beirut. There, on an October Sunday morning, 241 American men died in the explosion of a suicide truck inside the Marine enclave. The same morning, dozens of French military men died in a similar attack.

The tragedy of Beirut spread through the nation in the form of taps and flags folded three-corner. The questions it raised about the U.S. presence in Lebanon forced the eventual pullout of American troops.

Late in October, American forces swept across the Caribbean island of Grenada. Ostensible purpose: to insure the safety of 1,000 Americans. Grenadians welcomed the American action. But the press raised loud protests because reporters were not allowed to accompany U.S. troops.

Even beyond Beirut and Grenada, terror, strife and killings dominated the news. In September, a Soviet fighter shot down a Korean airliner carrying 269 civilians after it strayed over Soviet air space. The incident prompted a flood of condemnation worldwide. But no Soviet apologies were forthcoming, and relations between the Soviets and the United States deteriorated apace.

(continued next page)

Above, crowds press in on the funeral procession of
Benigno Aquino, Philippines opposition leader, who
stepped off an airplane in Manila and was shot to death.

Below, caskets of 14 South Korean officials killed by a
terrorist bomb in Rangoon, Burma, are massed for a
memorial service in Seoul, South Korea's capital city.

Violence ... and more

(from preceding page)

And more killings: In Rangoon, Burma, a terrorist bombing decimated the South Korean government; 14 of that nation's top officials were killed. In August, Philippine opposition leader Benigno Aquino was shot to death at the Manila airport after returning from a self-imposed three-year exile in the United States.

While violence marked American interests and attention overseas, other actions had quieter but equally far-reaching effects on the national consciousness: The Soviets broke off arms talks with the United States, while protests against nuclear weaponry mounted both in Europe and America.

On the domestic front, the economy, the weather and the fortunes of Washington politicos caught the attention of both the media and the public.

The weather — always a major story — demanded continuing coverage and concern; the snow, the flooding, the cold and drought, the hurricanes and the tornadoes made compelling local stories for almost every news outlet in the country. So, too, did the economy, still struggling to break out of the recessionary doldrums of the preceding year.

Meanwhile, the pace of the news accelerated.

Sally Ride became the first American woman in space; and the political hopefuls began their first tentative steps in the campaign leading to the presidential election in November 1984.

The American Cup left our shores for the first time in 132 years; and Red Soxer Carl Yastrzemski called it quits after 23 seasons.

The Brooklyn Bridge celebrated its 100th anniversary; and Boy George led the annual British rock invasion. Rita M. Lavelle swore she didn't do wrong as head of EPA's waste cleanup, but a jury disagreed.

And the news photographer was part of it all: recording it, reacting to it, getting the story, capturing the images, bringing the nation a clearer idea of the pressures that played upon us all and of the events that marked 1983 for better or worse.

In Bonn, West Germany, police use water cannons against cowering demonstrators. The protest was against the planned deployment of new cruise and Pershing II missiles in their country.

KARL-HEINZ KREIFELTS, ASSOCIATED PRESS

9

FIRST, MAGAZINE FEATURE, JAMES NACHTWEY, BLACK STAR FOR TIME

Above, a youngster swings on a former Somoza tank, left in a Managua park as a relic of the revolution. Below, Korean Americans attend a demonstration in New York City in September, to mourn the 269 persons who died in the Soviet destruction of Korean Air Lines Flight 007.

ROBERT MAASS, PHOTOREPORTERS, INC., FOR NEWSWEEK

Australia II (right) moves past
Liberty; after 132 years, the
America's Cup went abroad, victim
of a secret keel.

DAN ROOT, THE MISSOULIAN, MISSOULA, MONT.

NED A. VESPA, NEWSPAPERS, INC., MILWAUKEE, WIS.

James Watt resigned as Interior secretary in October 1983, after referring to members of a coal advisory commission as "a black . . . a woman, two Jews and a cripple." Three months earlier, Watt visited the Glacier National Park (above). Says Photographer Dan Root: "The image is of a man and a national treasure. He seems small in comparison."

The race for the Democratic nomination for the presidency got under way months before most people were giving it much thought. Among an octet of party hopefuls (right), Calif. Sen. Alan Cranston, who makes himself available to the media near the Milwaukee Art Center during his morning headstand.

RICH LIPSKI, UNITED PRESS INTERNATIONAL

President Ronald Reagan got up before an audience of
White House news photographers and said: "I've been
waiting years to do this." Photographer Rich Lipski's
quick reflexes and motor drive caught the presidential
gesture, even though, Lipski says, "I didn't know what he
was going to do."

At left, in one of two widely covered trips out of the
Vatican in 1983, Pope John Paul II addresses an audience
in Managua, Nicaragua.

13

Caribbean 'hoot'

The U.S. military establishment showed its muscle - and its attitude towards the press - when the Army's 82nd Airborne invaded the Caribbean island of Grenada late in October. The invasion followed the execution of Prime Minister Maurice Bishop. American troops overwhelmed a strong resistance from Cubans and retrieved more than 600 American medical students stranded on the island.

Most news agencies called the Grenadian invasion one of the top news stories of 1983. And Newsweek Magazine said it "would have been described as a textbook operation, if there had been any reporters along to witness it."

Eighteen Americans were killed. But the Marxist regime was wiped out. The immediate world

(Continued on Page 16)

Left, pre-dawn strike on Grenada.

Above, one of the 600 American
medical students to be airlifted out
of Grenada salutes American military
men as plane returns some of the
students to the United States.

Invasion

(Continued from Page 14)

reaction: dismay, denunciation. Grenadians, however, welcomed the Americans.

Biggest and continuing question arising out of the invasion came from the news media, whose spokesmen complained that the operation had been mounted without any combat reporters and photographers permitted to accompany the troops.

Some news photographers were on hand when the invasion began. Others eventually got on the island.

According to UPI's Tom Salyer, "Hundreds of members of the international press corps arrived in Bridgetown, Barbados, late on the first day of the invasion, anxious to cover . . .

"We sat. And sat. And yelled at the military . . . Two and a half days later, the first print media and TV pool was flown over for a quick visit."

Salyer's assessment of the Grenadian coverage: "A real hoot. No one knew from hour to hour what was happening, how we were to cover it. We had major logistical problems with film shipments and communications.

"All the shooting was on the run, no time to dally, because we had to play catch-up and show the effects of the invasion."

U.S. soldier (above) shares his canteen water with a suspected member of the People's Revolutionary Army.

Two American troopers (below) move a Cuban prisoner from a crowded police station behind the Point Salines airport to another area for questioning.

TOM SALYER, UNITED PRESS INTERNATIONAL

PAUL A. SCHMICK, THE WASHINGTON (D.C.) TIMES

TOM SALYER, UNITED PRESS INTERNATIONAL

Above, three men suspected of membership in the People's Revolutionary Army under guard. They were flushed from the hills surrounding St. George's, Grenada, three days after the United States invaded.

Below, compound in which prisoners were held awaiting interrogation by U.S. forces.

ARTHUR GRACE, TIME

SECOND PLACE, NEWSPAPER GENERAL NEWS, TOM SALYER, UNITED PRESS INTERNATIONAL

VICKI VALERIO, THE PHILADELPHIA (PA.) INQUIRER

Post-invasion

Above, a week after the invasion, three U.S. soldiers are stripped down for a swim in the Grenada surf, all the while keeping their M-16 automatic weapons in easy reach.

Right, Ranger Cpl. Chuck Smith sits under an American flag, waiting return to the States. He's in a staging area near the Point Salines Airfield. Photographer Vicki Valerio, who chose to miss an outgoing press plane to make the picture, says she spent days on the island, sleeping on a hotel floor, going without a change of clothing.

Above, three men suspected of membership in the People's Revolutionary Army under guard. They were flushed from the hills surrounding St. George's, Grenada, three days after the United States invaded.

Below, compound in which prisoners were held awaiting interrogation by U.S. forces.

SECOND PLACE, NEWSPAPER GENERAL NEWS, TOM SALYER, UNITED PRESS INTERNATIONAL

VICKI VALERIO, THE PHILADELPHIA (PA.) INQUIRER

Post-invasion

Above, a week after the invasion, three U.S. soldiers are stripped down for a swim in the Grenada surf, all the while keeping their M-16 automatic weapons in easy reach.

Right, Ranger Cpl. Chuck Smith sits under an American flag, waiting return to the States. He's in a staging area near the Point Salines Airfield. Photographer Vicki Valerio, who chose to miss an outgoing press plane to make the picture, says she spent days on the island, sleeping on a hotel floor, going without a change of clothing.

LOU KRASKY, ASSOCIATED PRESS

CINDY BURNHAM, THE FAYETTEVILLE, N.C., TIMES

Above, the expressions show how these members of the 82nd Airborne feel on arrival at Fort Bragg, N.C.

Left, Craig Van Winkle gets a welcome home kiss from wife Carmen in a rain-soaked reunion. In the middle? Daughter Felicia.

Bloody Beirut

The Associated Press called 1983 "the bloodiest year for American servicemen since Vietnam." Most of that blood was spilled early on an October Sunday morning in Lebanon.

Marines of the U.S. peacekeeping force in Beirut were asleep in their barracks when an explosive-laden truck surged past guards and into the military compound, where it blew up, collapsing the barracks and killing 241 Marines. Dozens of French soldiers died in a similar attack.

During the next few days, the names of the dead Marines were made known. And with those names, all across the nation, the shock of the loss came home.

President Reagan's immediate reaction: U.S. forces would stay in Lebanon to provide stability so that the country's shaky government could go forward to reach compromises among the many disparate and belligerent factions.

In the days following the massacre, U.S. involvement in Lebanon expanded. American jets went in against entrenched Syrian forces. One pilot died; another airman was captured.

But American public reaction was growing, and the handwriting on the wall was clear: Get out.

On their arrival in Lebanon, American Marines dug in and adopted pets. Above, a stray kitten takes over in one military position. Below, a Marine takes a break by playing keepaway with the company mascot. Says Photographer Chas Cancellare, "Pictures like this were harder to find following the bombing!"

HONORABLE MENTION, NEWSPAPER FEATURE, RICK T. WILKING, UNITED PRESS INTERNATIONAL

Above, using balls and a golf club sent from the United States by his father, a Marine chips from sand in front of military position near the Lebanese university.

Below, a Marine takes a shower during a rare Condition One, in which troopers didn't have to wear flak jackets, helmets, or carry their arms. As the autumn wore on, this kind of luxury became almost non-existent.

NORMAN Y. LONO, PHILADELPHIA (PA.) DAILY NEWS

Bloody Beirut

Right, headquarters building following the Beirut bombing. Below, rescuers prepare to lower a Marine on a stretcher. He was trapped in the wreckage of the command post.

CHAS CANCELLARE, UNITED PRESS INTERNATIONAL

HONORABLE MENTION, NEWSPAPER SPOT NEWS, BILL FOLEY, ASSOCIATED PRESS

Above, a clenched fist signals a trapped paratrooper pinned beneath the rubble. Left, a Marine, his leg deeply torn from the explosion, is carried away for emergency medical treatment.

Bloody Beirut

Rescue worker holds the hand of a Marine buried in the rubble.

Bodies of dead Marines are covered by troopers in the
headquarters compound.

Beirut aftermath

Above, Robert and Sandra Cole, of Ludlow Falls, Ohio, weep at the funeral of their son, Marine Pfc. Marc Cole, 19, who died in the Beirut bombing. Says Photographer Bill Waugh, "After a few frames I began to feel the loss of their son as they were feeling it. I stopped shooting and began to pray with them."

Right, Mrs. Aletha Kimm, mother of Marine Edward Kimm, grieves at his graveside in Adair, Iowa. Photographer David Peterson says he was "amazed at her strength."

OPPOSITE PAGE: Above, in Painsville, Ohio, a sobbing Mishleen Earle embraces the casket of her husband, Navy Corpsman Bryan L. Earle. They had been married six days.

Below, in Palmdale, Calif., a grieving mother, Donna Phelps, pays a final tribute to her son, Donny Vallone, Jr.

HONORABLE MENTION, NEWSPAPER GENERAL NEWS, DAVID I. ANDERSEN, THE PLAIN DEALER (CLEVELAND, OHIO)

SECOND PLACE, NEWSPAPER FEATURE PICTURE STORY, MICHAEL BRYANT, SAN JOSE (CALIF.) MERCURY NEWS

On patrol at a coffee plantation near the Nicaraguan-Honduran border, a Sandinista Army reservist squad leader guards against Contra attack.

'Liquid, chaotic'

It was a year of no change in Central America, where revolution and counter-revolution ebbed and flowed. Events in other parts of the world drew public attention away from the agony and strife in Nicaragua, El Salvador, and Guatemala.

Still, journalists were going into Central American front lines that photojournalist J. Ross Baughman called "liquid, chaotic, and very dangerous."

Writing in the Columbia Journalism Review, Baughman commented on the death of

Newsweek photographer John Hoagland in El Salvador March 16:

"Neither the people in New York nor the people on the scene seem yet to have grasped a grim fact — that more journalists have been killed or wounded in Central America (21 in the past five years) than in any other conflict of its size or duration. This is not because the fighting there is any more dangerous than in other wars, but because of a new style of war correspondence that actually pushes reporters to take more risks than the soldiers on either side."

MARI A. SCHAEFER, TUCSON (ARIZ.) CITIZEN

Photographer Mari A. Schaefer was part of a team making massive reportage on the plight of Guatemalans. Above, in Valparaiso, the military supervises training of the civil patrol, using sticks as substitutes for rifles.

Below, the commander of a guerrilla force fighting the Sandinista government in Nicaragua takes the point for his patrol in the mountainous regions of the country.

DAVID LEESON, THE TIMES-PICAYUNE (NEW ORLEANS, LA.)

RICHARD MARSHALL, THE ITHACA (N.Y.) JOURNAL

Off they go

Anti-nuclear demonstrators were hauled away singly and in bunches all across the United States and Europe. The largest protest movement swept across Western Europe, where "Hot Autumn" campaigns were launched in opposition to the deployment of new Pershing 2 and Tomahawk cruise missiles.

At home, the nuclear freeze movement grew as demonstrators sought negotiations to end the arms race and ban nuclear arms. But U.S.-Soviet talks came to a halt when the Russians walked out. And the protests subsided.

This woman scaled a fence at the Seneca Army Depot in Romulus, N.Y., in August. Nearly 2,000 women were protesting the suspected storage and shipment of Pershing 2 cruise missiles at the depot. Some 200 were arrested.

Protester is carried off (left) during demonstration at Offutt Air Force Base, Nebr., in April. Photographer Paul Iwanaga's assessment: "Demonstrators and military personnel were cooperative with each other. Protesters ... allowed themselves to be escorted, or, in this case, dragged to an Air Force bus."

LEFT, PAUL IWANAGA, THE KANSAS CITY (MO.) TIMES

In Philadelphia, an anti-nuclear demonstrator is dragged away from a corporate office after he handcuffed himself to the front door.

In suburban Chicago, a woman is dragged away after protesters tried to block traffic entering the Northrop plant. Thirty-seven were arrested.

Protesters

TIM THOMPSON, THE OAKLAND PRESS (PONTIAC, MICH.)

In Pontiac, Mich., a 78-year-old minister, Maurice McCrackin (above), is carried into district court. He was one of 10 persons arrested for anti-nuclear demonstrations outside a plant in which cruise missile engines are built.

At Vandenberg Air Force Base, Calif., a 79-year-old woman, Terry Mead (below), is frisked after protesters tried to block a main gate. More than 200 of the 1,000 demonstrators were arrested, then released.

MICHAEL RONDOU, LONG BEACH (CALIF.) PRESS-TELEGRAM

Good times ?

Slowly, slowly, the hard times waned, and the good times seemed not only possible, but probable. After 17 months of recession and an unemployment rate that touched 11 percent, the American economy began to turn around in 1983.

Most of the numbers were positive: industry was operating at 80 percent of capacity, up from 66 percent in 1982. The inflation rate rose less than 4 percent. Retail sales were surging, housing starts were up, and the gross national product was growing.

And yet, much of the hard times remained. Nine million Americans were still out of work. The deficit hovered around $200 billion, and the specter of higher interest rates threatened the tenuous and tentative sense of optimism creeping across the nation.

Some 4,500 persons waited in the rain to see President Reagan at a national joint labor-industry conference on dislocated workers in Pittsburgh, Pa. But the president left without confronting the crowd or its concerns.

Above, when a Reynolds Metals aluminum plant in Longview, Wash., announced that job applications would be accepted for the first time in two years, 1,200 job seekers lined up in the rain for a chance to apply.

At right, a back-packer who identified himself as "Shotgun" came to Monterey, Calif., from Montana, looking for work.

Hard times, good times

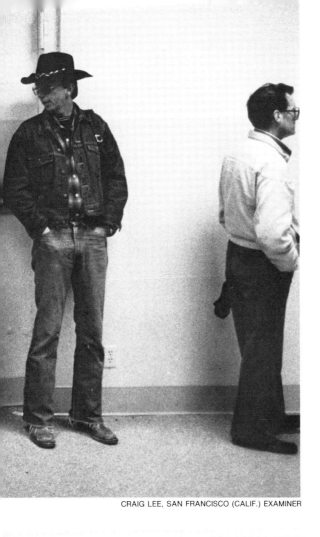

Left, men stand in line for their turn at the annual Thanksgiving dinner at St. Anthony's Church in San Francisco's tenderloin district. Below, another line: college graduates wait to talk with corporate recruiters in a talent search sponsored by the Philadelphia Chamber of Commerce.

Good times, at last

Fourteen months after General Motors closed its plant in Fremont, Calif., Fred Bobbitt returned to work on an auto assembly line. One problem: the line was 1,600 miles away, in Oklahoma City. But it was a job — and Bobbitt jubilantly greeted another re-located Californian on his first day back at work.

Leave the driving ...

It was not a good year for labor, including the 12,500 employees of Greyhound Bus Lines who went on strike early in November rather than accept deep cuts in wages and benefits.

The company hired 1,300 non-union replacements and eventually resumed service. But before the strike was settled, picket-line violence was recorded all across the country.

In Salinas, Calif. (right), a shop steward for 38 striking Greyhound workers blocks the path of the first bus to leave the city after the strike began. He was among four pickets arrested.

Below, striking Greyhound employees picket Minneapolis, Minn., terminal.

RICHARD GREEN, SALINAS CALIFORNIAN

MARLIN LEVISON, MINNEAPOLIS (MINN.) STAR AND TRIBUNE

THOMAS E. LANDERS, THE BOSTON (MASS.) GLOBE

Above, Boston, Mass., bus driver waits behind egg-splattered windshield while police try to clear demonstrators out of his path. The bus was detained 1 1/2 hours; 51 pickets were arrested.

Below, pickets in Washington, D.C., yell and gesture as non-union drivers get buses rolling.

LAWRENCE LAMBER, THE WASHINGTON (D.C.) TIMES

JIM GENSHEIMER, THE LOUISVILLE (KY.) COURIER-JOURNAL

MAGAZINE PHOTOGRAPHER OF THE YEAR JAMES NACHTWEY, BLACK STAR FOR TIME

They still dream

These three photographs were made as 300,000 people marched on Washington, D.C., in August to commemorate the 20th anniversary of the civil rights march led by Martin Luther King, Jr. — a march that was climaxed with King's "I have a dream" speech.

At left, marchers mass at the Lincoln Memorial. Lower left, Coretta Scott King, widow of the black leader, is led to the head of a line of marchers. Lower right, a study of some of the march participants.

The AIDS story

By Steve Ringman
San Francisco Chronicle
Newspaper Photographer of the Year

In 1981, four men in the Los Angeles area died of a rare cancer called Kaposi's Sarcoma. These were the first identified cases of AIDS syndrome — a strange, mystifying disease among gay people.

We had hysteria. Some of my own co-workers refused to cover the story, or would only shoot AIDS patients from a long distance or through a window.

The San Francisco Chronicle has a gay reporter who was very instrumental in helping our team cover the story. We spent three days at San Francisco General Hospital in a wing devoted entirely to the care of people with AIDS.

We spent most of our time getting to know the people, and in time they made the choice to let us into their lives and allow me to record their fight against death.

This was, obviously, a very difficult assignment for me. Yet it was a real challenge, and a rewarding story to be a part of. I think our report helped change people's emotion from panic to compassion. They could read about and, which is unique to photojournalism, see and feel the patients' suffering.

GHTING
UR LIVES

FIRST PLACE, NEWSPAPER FEATURE STORY, STEVE RINGMAN, SAN FRANCISCO (CALIF.) CHRONICLE

A candlelight march in downtown San Francisco massed support for AIDS victims. Says Photographer Ringman, "San Francisco's very strong gay community has continually rallied and been outspoken politically in an effort to get the funds for AIDS care and research."

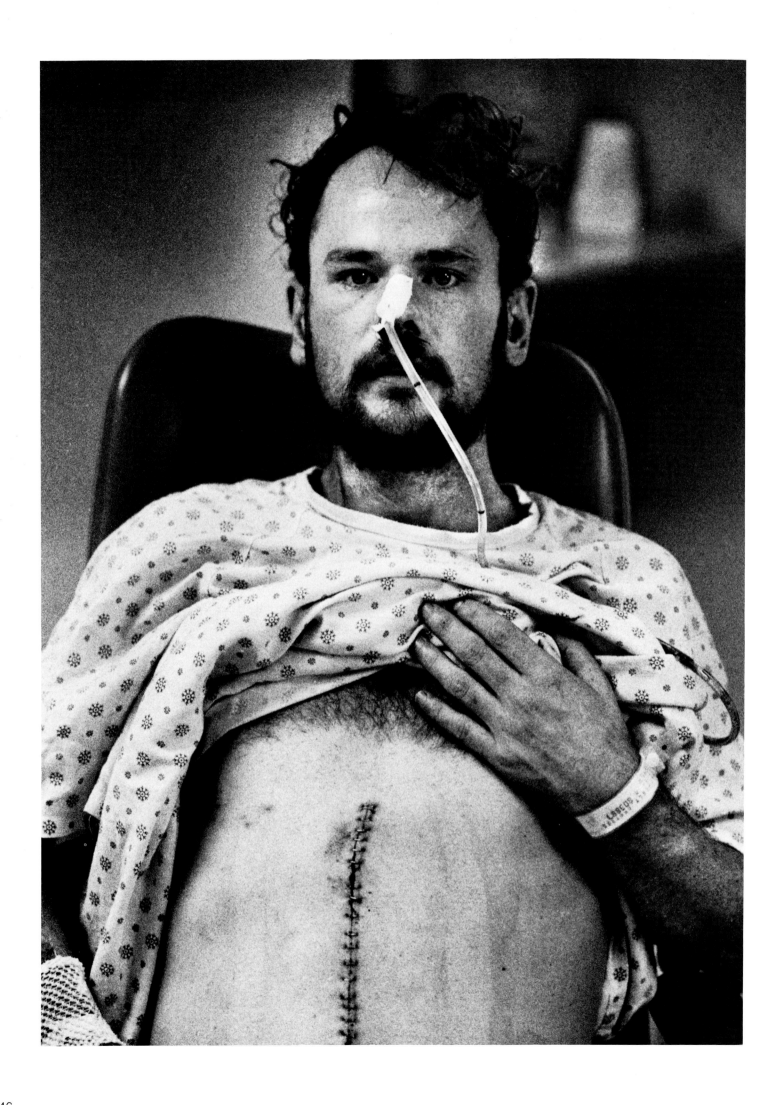

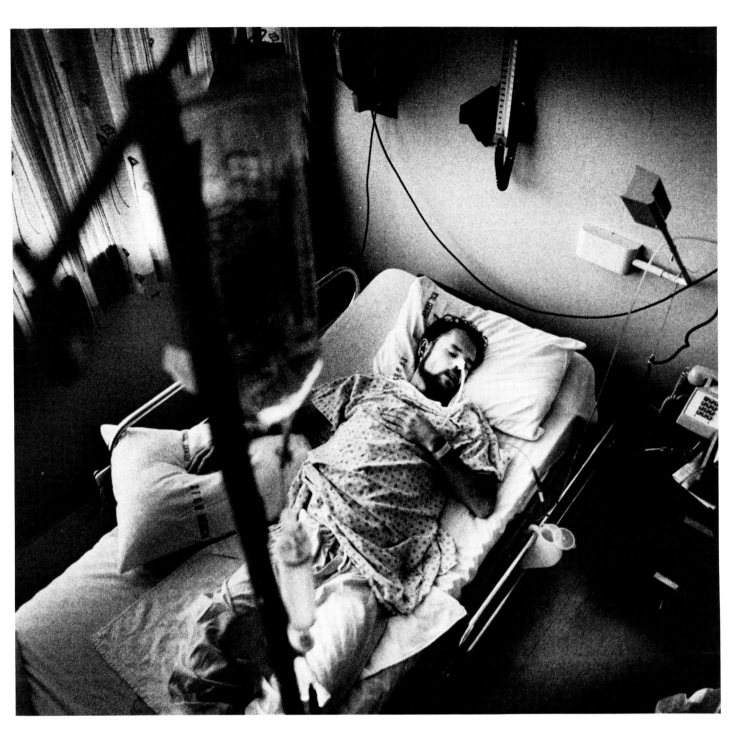

Deotis McMather, 27, died faster than any of his unlucky fellow patients in AIDS Ward 5B. A week into his stay, doctors determined he had ideopathic thrombocytopenic purpura, one of the bizarre diseases associated with AIDS. Because it had inflamed many of his abdominal organs, physicians cut out McMather's spleen and parts of his liver and stomach. Two weeks later, McMather's usually sad disposition turned grim. "I don't want to be . . . a drain on other people," he said. His condition worsened; he was put on a respirator. Finally, McMather asked nurses to take out the breathing tubes, and he died.

The AIDS story

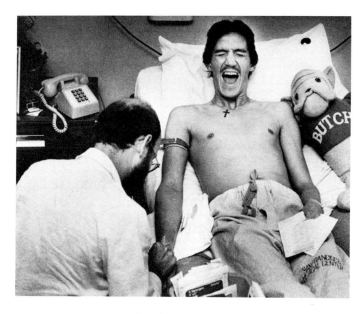

Bruce Schneider reacts when a nurse puts a needle into his arm. His illness was diagnosed as pneumocystis carinii pneumonia. Average patient with AIDS lives 10 months after diagnosis. "This is like being on death row," says Schneider.

Schneider turned to religion in an effort to deal with the trauma of his illness.

The AIDS story

Reports Photographer Ringman, "When you have AIDS, the thought of a destroyed immune system never leaves. It is haunting. You become a victim of your fears about suffering and death. And you are alone."

DAVID L. POKRESS, NEWSDAY (LONG ISLAND, N.Y., RIGHT)

Here's what a two-foot snowfall (right) does to a car rental lot in Denver, Colo. Above, results of another two feet of new-fallen snow, this time on Long Island.

Nature unleashed

The vagaries of the elements are a basic in the diet of the news media. The weather is good for a feature picture, even on a good day. But when assorted disasters hit — and hit they do, inevitably — the news photographer functions.

KEN PAPALEO, ROCKY MOUNTAIN NEWS (DENVER, COLO

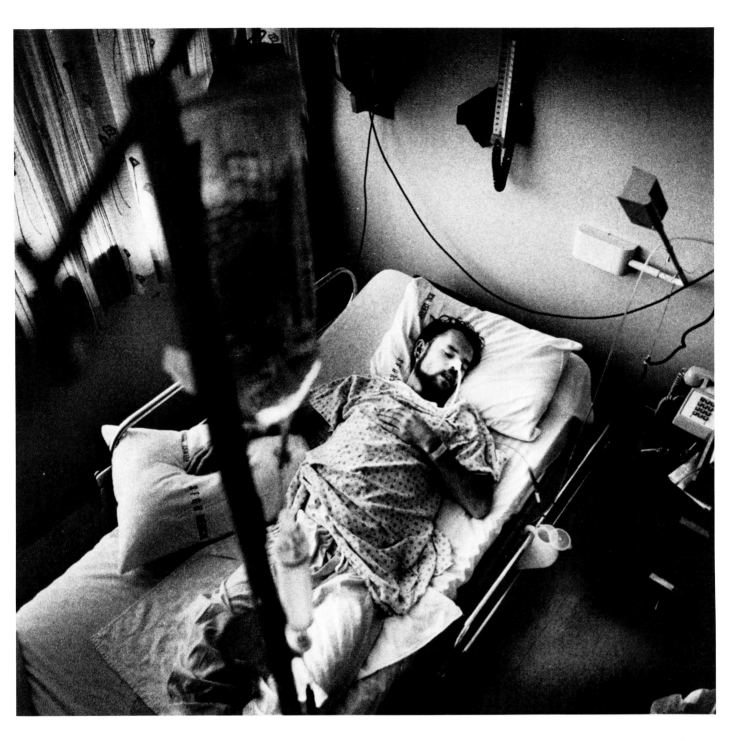

Deotis McMather, 27, died faster than any of his unlucky fellow patients in AIDS Ward 5B. A week into his stay, doctors determined he had ideopathic thrombocytopenic purpura, one of the bizarre diseases associated with AIDS. Because it had inflamed many of his abdominal organs, physicians cut out McMather's spleen and parts of his liver and stomach. Two weeks later, McMather's usually sad disposition turned grim. "I don't want to be . . . a drain on other people," he said. His condition worsened; he was put on a respirator. Finally, McMather asked nurses to take out the breathing tubes, and he died.

The AIDS story

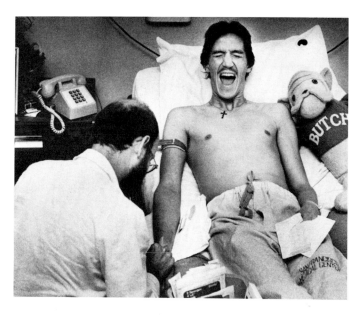

Bruce Schneider reacts when a nurse puts a needle into his arm. His illness was diagnosed as pneumocystis carinii pneumonia. Average patient with AIDS lives 10 months after diagnosis. "This is like being on death row," says Schneider.

Schneider turned to religion in an effort to deal with the trauma of his illness.

The AIDS story

Reports Photographer Ringman, "When you have AIDS, the thought of a destroyed immune system never leaves. It is haunting. You become a victim of your fears about suffering and death. And you are alone."

SIG BOKALDERS, PADDOCK PUBLICATIONS (ARLINGTON HEIGHTS, ILL.)

'Worst ever'

The midwinter triangle of man vs. car vs. snow is played out on the day of Christmas Eve in the Chicago area (extreme left). Adding to the problem: temperatures of 25 below zero. In Minnesota, says Photographer Marlin Levison, "the only way to survive winter is to stick together," as these motorists (near left) are doing during an April snow storm.

Photographer Bradley Clift recorded a winter front moving out of Illinois late in December. It was, he says, "the worst winter ever in the Midwest" (and the deciding factor in Clift's decision to move to the East Coast.)

MARLIN LEVISON, MINNEAPOLIS (MINN.) STAR AND TRIBUNE

BRADLEY CLIFT, THE DAILY PANTAGRAPH (BLOOMINGTON, ILL.)

PAUL S. HOWELL, THE TIMES (SHREVEPORT, LA.)

Photographer Paul Howell went to an elementary school to shoot winners of a science fair. But, says Howell, "Before I ever shot the winners, a tornado was spotted." The picture that resulted (above) was not a drill.

A windstorm whipped through central Minnesota in July. Photographer Steve Woit says he didn't feel he had captured the impact of the storm until he saw the four daughters of Ralph and Kathy Kalthoff (below) in the rubble of their St. Martin farm buildings.

STEVE WOIT, ST. CLOUD (MINN.) TIMES

BORIS YARO, LOS ANGELES (CALIF.) TIMES (ALL PHOTOS)

Now, *that's* a wave!

"This sequence," says Photographer Boris Yaro, "is my best attempt to tell our readers what a big wave looks like." Taking the brunt of the water's force are three home owners – and a fireman attempting to put plywood over doors and windows during a storm.

"The wave was as unexpected in size and intensity to me as it was to the men who were caught by it," recalls Yaro. Total injuries: one cut thumb.

Going home

Three months after floods and winds battered their Illinois farm, Robert and Doreen Wear and their grandson (right) head for home and the massive job of rebuilding. In Costa Mesa, Calif. (below), the rainfall was the heaviest they'd seen in 22 years. Homes were evacuated, roadways paralyzed, and traffic stood still — except for Jim Buchmiller and his 10-speed bike.

JOHN BADMAN, ALTON (ILL.) TELEGRAPH

CHRISTINE COTTER, LOS ANGELES (CALIF.) TIMES

Left, motorists navigate through water that accumulated on a freeway in Pueblo, Colo. As the high water stalled the vehicles, Photographer Chandler reports, teenagers pushed the disabled autos to dry ground. Cost: about $10 a car. Neither flood nor foul play befell 82-year-old Roy Bray (below). The would-be Washington fisherman got out of his truck to check a trailer problem, and everything rolled into the river. Another outdoorsman helped winch out Bray's rig.

EMMETT BLUM, THE TIMES-PICAYUNE (NEW ORLEANS, LA.)

Heavy spring floods rolled through eight parishes in the New Orleans area. In Slidell, La. (above), residents load sandbags into boats in an effort to protect their homes from rising water.

Two Northbridge, R.I., firemen (below) find themselves in trouble when their boat begins shipping water during a rescue mission. They eventually saved the woman on the branch above them; she had been stranded when her canoe capsized.

FRANK VISGATIS III, THE WOONSOCKET (R.I.) CALL

THOMAS KELSEY, LOS ANGELES (CALIF.) TIMES

Huntington Beach, Calif., firemen evacuate a mobile home park (above), as worst flooding in 40 years hits Orange County. Photographer Thomas Kelsey spent more time aiding victims and firemen than he did with his cameras.

When high water is inevitable, relax and enjoy it (below). This is winter flooding in Hattiesburg, Miss.

STAN BADZ, THE CLARION-LEDGER (JACKSON, MISS.)

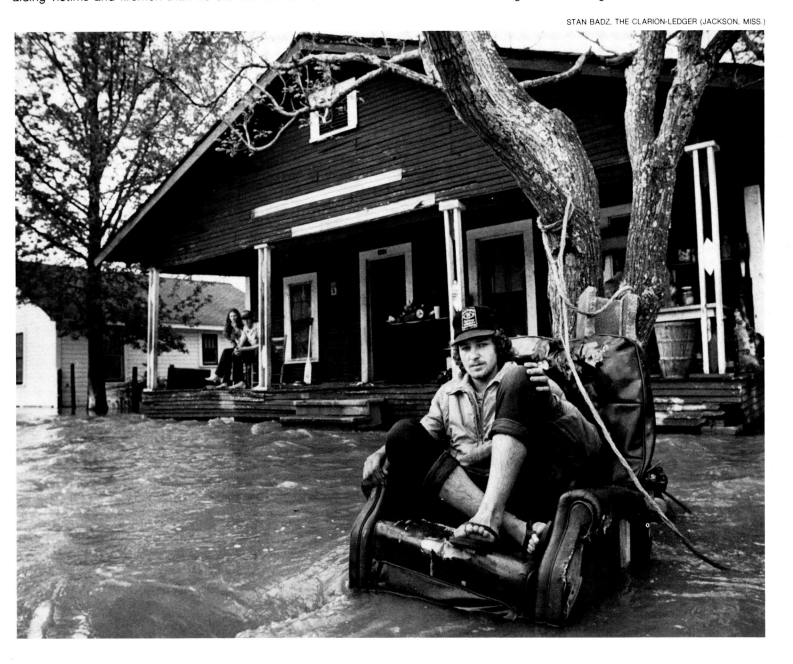

A Turkish mother (above) mourns her five children, buried alive in an October earthquake that registered 7.1 on the Richter scale. The quake leveled 147 villages and killed 1,836 persons. In May, commercial and residential buildings in Coalinga, Calif. (left), were destroyed in an earthquake with a Richter intensity of 6.7. Miraculously, says Photographer Paul Kuroda, there were no injuries, although most of the residences in the city were either destroyed or sustained major structural damage.

THIRD PLACE, NEWSPAPER SPOT NEWS, TOM VAN DYKE, SAN JOSE (CALIF.) MERCURY NEW

In Alviso, Calif. (above), residents throw their bodies against a rapidly deteriorating levee in a hopeless effort to protect their homes from rain-swollen marsh water. Says Photographer Tom Van Dyke, "It represents the utter futility and desperation of something that had begun as a hopeful community effort." A few hours later, the entire town was under four to eight feet of water.

CHARLIE LEIGHT, COLUMBIA (MO.) DAILY TRIBUNE

Community effort paid off (right) in Hartsburg, Mo., where volunteers came from miles away to help patch a break in a flood levee. They stayed on the job, reports Photographer Charlie Leight, until the flood receded.

Naked and bleeding, John Swan, 38, of Quincy, Mass., (above) is pulled from the water off Malibu Beach by a Boston police officer who is leaning from the helicopter of a TV weatherman.

Nogales, Ariz., police officers (below) use garden hose in rescue of a 32-year-old victim of an epileptic seizure from the Santa Cruz River. Incident occurred during the worst Arizona flooding in modern history.

ALAN BERNER, THE SEATTLE (WASH.) TIMES

Suffering from hypothermia, an exhausted Jim Gillick (left) is plucked from Puget Sound by seaplane pilot Jim Taylor. Plane was chartered by The Seattle Times to cover Coast Guard search for Gillick, who had been riding a water cycle in the Sound. Photographer Alan Berner accompanied the pilot, who spotted Gillick struggling in the water. When the plane landed, Berner hopped onto a float, and the pilot assisted the waterlogged Gillick to safety.

Below, a highway patrolman buoys up a woman who attempted suicide by jumping into the Hudson River.

MICHAEL LEACH, THE NEW YORK DAILY NEWS

FIRST PLACE, NEWSPAPER SPOT NEWS, JORGE DURAN, FREELANCE FOR UNITED PRESS INTERNATIONAL

In Mexico City, a young girl who was part of closing ceremonies of the World Youth Soccer Cup games runs screaming with her hair afire after gas-filled balloons exploded in the Azteca Stadium.

Above, a California Highway Patrol helicopter crew searches for bodies after a cruiser was overturned by a large wave along the coast just north of the Golden Gate Bridge.

Below, the Cathedral Hill Hotel fire, ignited by a Christmas tree in the lobby, killed three people in San Francisco and caused more than $1 million in damage. This woman was evacuated safely from the ninth floor.

In Simi Valley, Calif. (below), police officer arrests a man later charged with discharging a firearm inside the city.

Below, Secret Service agents, riding shotgun on presidential limo, leave the Augusta National Golf Course after an intruder broke though a gate, took hostage in the pro shop, and demanded to see President Reagan.

BOB DAWSON, THE ENTERPRISE (SIMI VALLEY, CALIF.)

In Los Angeles (below), officers draw down on man who ran out of barricaded building during an armed robbery, before learning he was the victim.

BORIS YARO, LOS ANGELES (CALIF.) TIMES

In Miami (left), police surround a robbery suspect in the upper deck of the Orange Bowl stadium.

FREDERIC LARSON, SAN FRANCISCO (CALIF). CHRONICLE

Photographer Frederic Larson staked out for two hours to record suspects in a bank robbery being arrested (above) as they attempt their getaway in a taxicab.

Below, police officers in Upland, Calif., search for a man involved in a neighborhood shooting spree.

PAUL E. RODRIGUEZ, CLAREMONT (CALIF.) COURIER

Left above, a Denver policeman confronts John Hall, who jumped out of his pickup truck after a minor accident and threatened other motorists with a knife. At right, Hall is arrested after he tossed his knife and collapsed on road.

Despondent after losing his job, an unidentified youth (below) fatally stabs an off-duty policeman in Quezon City, Philippines. The officer had emptied his revolver at the young man during a chase. Onlookers, who had armed themselves with stones, were helpless.

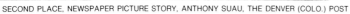

Canon Photo Essayist Award —

Streets of the lost

A compeling story of street kids in Seattle, Wash., won the Canon Photo Essayist Award in 1983. The story was photographed by Mary Ellen Mark, Archive Agency for Life, which ran an extended essay on the problems of runaway kids in the Pacific Northwest.

Here are excerpts from the Life story that accompanied Mark's photographs:

"Every city in America has them. There are a thousand in Seattle alone — homeless teenagers who use only their first names to hide their identities . . . a new generation of runaways and abandoned children struggling to survive on their own.

"Each year, more than one million American youngsters betwen 11 and 17 run away. More than half are girls, and the majority are never reported missing by their apparently indifferent families . . . most are fleeing turbulent households racked by conflict, violence, neglect, and — in a disturbingly high percent of cases — sexual abuse. But a growing number are casualties of the prolonged recession.

"Each year, according to federal records, some 5,000 unidentified teenagers end up in unmarked graves, and another 50,000 simply disappear. No one knows what happens to them. Too young to get jobs or to receive welfare, a significant majority resort to theft, peddling drugs and prostitution to support themselves.

" . . . In Seattle, where 6,000 runaways are reported each year, there are only The Shelter, a single eight-bed facility, and a few impoverished church-run programs like the St. Dismas Center to provide help. Fending for themselves, most street kids spend the nights in abandoned cars, steam-bath cubicles, under bridges, and even in cemeteries.

"To answer their needs, many of Seattle's street kids risk arrest — and worse — by becoming prostitutes, what they call 'turning dates.' Boys and girls, who stash their clothes in bus station lockers during the day, drift near the waterfront's Pike Street Market and wait for offers . . .

"Tragically, trafficking in drugs is considered a step up — street kids find it less degrading than prostitution — None of these kids can go to school — even if they wanted to. They have no permanent address, and schools will not admit them . . . .

"The National Runaway Switchboard lists 7,000 agencies around the country that counsel or help youngsters in various ways, and approximately 300 shelters provide emergency housing for runaways. Congress allocated $21 million in 1983 to fund hotlines and teenager shelters, but by its own estimate, those facilities serve only 45,000 kids a year, a mere fraction of the needy. More help is required . . . ."

Above, friends Rat, 16 (left), and Mike, (17) insist they have this Colt .45 only for defense against men who try to pick them up or rob them. Below left, window is the only entry into the spooky abandoned hotel where Mike and Rat sleep. Below right, Rat gives the finger to a man who ignored his begging.

Streets of the lost

In a crash pad for runaways, this young dealer is injecting a 14-year-old customer with MDA (methylene dioxy amphetamine).

Left, a homeless boy collapses in agonizing spasms; medics speculated his problem was drug-related. Center, the girls call the boy on the bed their "popcorn pimp" because he is only 18. Right, James, 18, sleeps under a waterfront viaduct.

Dark-haired Patti, 16, waited until her victim's pimp was out of sight and then jumped the girl because she never returned a borrowed jacket. Shaken but unhurt, the girl finds her pimp, who calls the cops. Minutes later, Patti was arrested, cited for simple assault, and released. Reported Life: "Like many runaways, (Patti) learned violence at home and doesn't hesitate to use it — even though she's now four months pregnant — to settle all disputes."

Streets of the lost

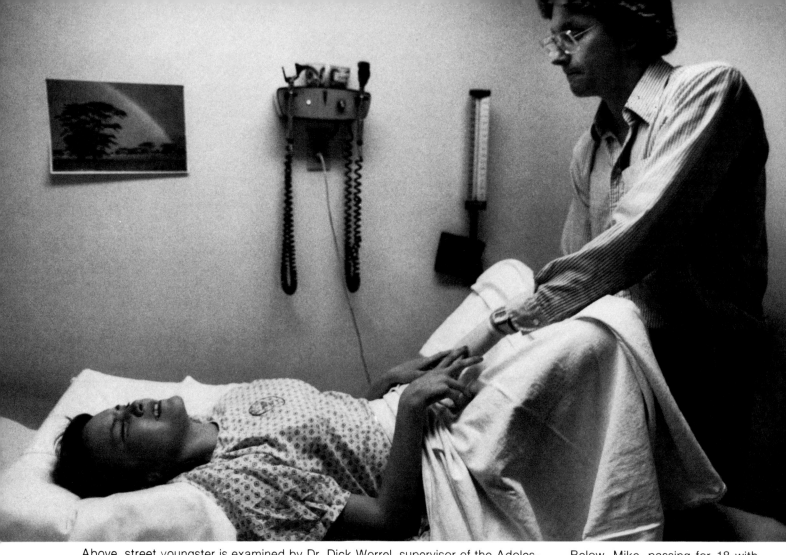

Above, street youngster is examined by Dr. Dick Worrel, supervisor of the Adolescent Free Clinic, operated by the University of Washington Medical School. He diagnosed her severe pelvic inflammation as chlamydia, a form of gonorrhea.

Below, Mike, passing for 18 with fake identification, earns $30 a week by selling plasma.

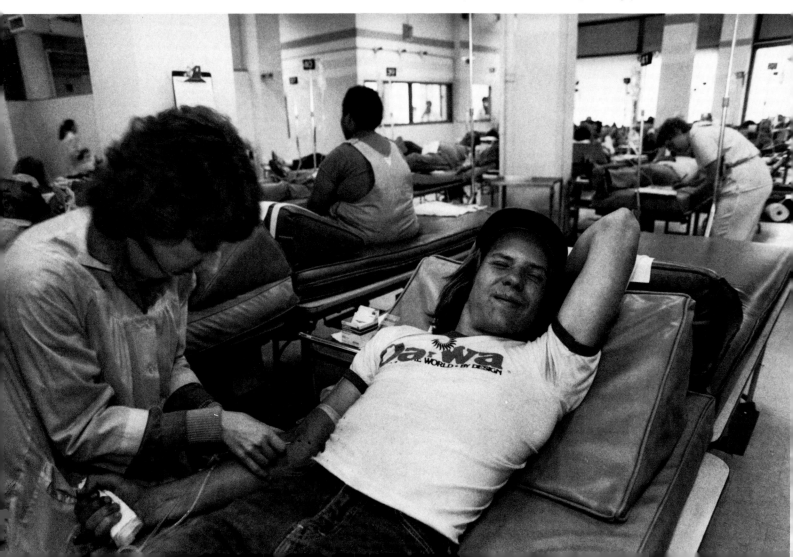

Above, Jackie (center) is 12 and a recent runaway. The only clothes she owns are on her back. On her second day on the street, she was befriended by these two flanking her; but she drifted out of their control.

Left, Laurie, 14, says a middle-aged doctor promised her $80, then sexually abused her, then reneged on the payment. She left Seattle to live with a Christian group in another part of the state.

Streets of the lost

Above, young woman with her child and stuffed bear is a retired street person who still frequents the Pike Street area to see her friends.

Above, Patti on Pike Street with her friend, Bobbi, 16, who has an 11-month-old baby boy and is pregnant with another child. Below, Bobbi cuddles her son, whom she leaves on the street for as long as 10 hours unattended.

Right, Candy, 17 (with baseball cap), and Paula, 19, are lovers and part of the corps of lesbian street kids who also turn tricks for survival money.

Streets of the lost

Boy on the left is known on the street as "White Junior". His pal is Justin, also 15. They command as much as $300 a "date," they say. After a particularly good night, both boys spent $300 each on their own "ghetto blaster" radio-cassette players.

Lauri, 14, and her friend, Teresa, 15, are just two Pike Street pavement dwellers.

Erin, 14, has been arrested twice for prostitution. Her probation order states that she must live with her family, not on the streets. But the girl and her stepfather argue. "He doesn't want me around," she says.

Right, 84-year-old Ed Jackson caresses a small visitor to the nursing home where Jackson lives. Below, John and Brenda Swaleson and son Lloyd, 5, encourage each other on their arrival in Spokane, Wash. They had come from Montana, looking for work in the Pacific Northwest.

FIRST PLACE, NEWSPAPER PORTRAIT/PERSONALITY, JIMI LOTT, SPOKANE (WASH.) REVIEW AND CHRONICLE

THIRD PLACE, NEWSPAPER PHOTOGRAPHER OF THE YEAR, JOHN KAPLAN, SPOKANE (WASH.) REVIEW AND CHRONICLE

ARTHUR VASSY, THE DAILY SOUTHTOWN ECONOMIST (CHICAGO, ILL.)

Left, in Chicago, a woman enfolds her child as she watches firemen battle a blaze in her apartment building. Below, in Immokalee, Fla., Sam and Marie Miller live in a wooden shack where they care for eight "adopted" kids — relatives' children, for the most part — on Sam's $316 monthly disability check. Says Sam, "The Lord dealt bountifully with me."

HONORABLE MENTION, NEWSPAPER PORTRAIT/PERSONALITY, CAROL GUZY, THE MIAMI (FLA.) HERALD

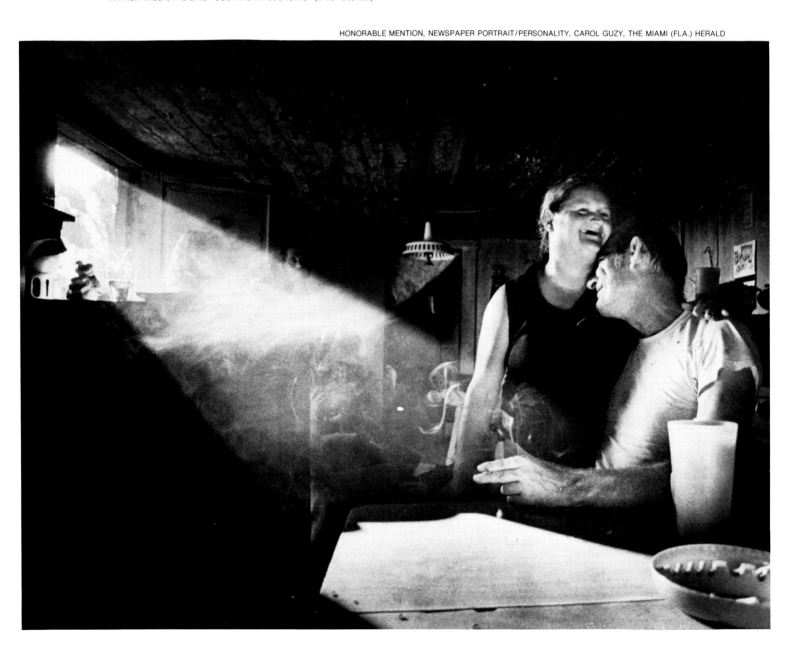

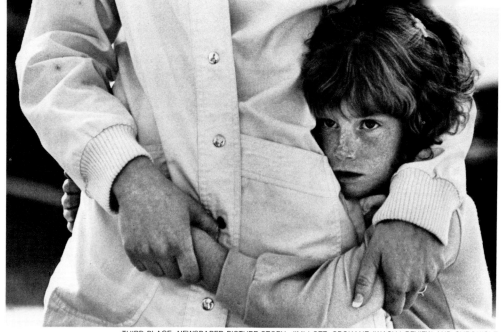

A young girl in Challis, Idaho, clutches her mother after a major earthquake shook the tiny town, killing two children. Says Photographer Jimi Lott, "This was, with no question, a media event. I've never seen so many press people in such a small town."

Family members console each other at the funeral services for Brian Orchard, the first police officer killed in Spokane, Wash., in 54 years.

On Memorial Day, Mrs. Dorris Fielder embraces the tombstone of her husband, Cecil, veteran of three wars. This photograph was a part of the portfolio for which Photographer Anthony Suau won the Pulitzer Prize for feature photography.

Opposite page: Florence Thompson, Dorothea Lange's "Migrant Mother," is comforted by her son in her final days.

Above, President Reagan breaks from Secret Service agents to work the crowd in Williamsburg, Va. Right, Mr. T, star of "The A Team," gets a lapful of First Lady. The occasion: a preview of White House Christmas decor.

His third year

President Ronald Reagan came into the last half of his first term in 1983. It was a year in which the nation's income rose while unemployment fell, a year in which eight Democrats hit the road seeking the chance to run against Reagan in 1984.

Reagan had a multitude of concerns: Soviets broke off arms talks; U.S. Marines were massacred in Beirut; American troops invaded the island of Grenada.

As the year closed, Time named Reagan one of its two Men of the Year (with Yuri Andropov), saying that "For all their angry rhetoric, the two superpowers have been extraordinarily careful to avoid any direct military confrontation."

With Japan's Emperor Hirohito at his
left, President Reagan gets a smiling
glance from his wife during
ceremonies in Tokyo.

England's Queen Elizabeth broke up President Reagan at
an affair in San Francisco near the end of a rain-drenched
tour. Said the Queen, "I knew before we came that we
have exported many of our traditions to the United States,
but I had not realized that weather was one of them."

Long, long trail

The year was still young when the pulling and hauling started among those hoping to nail down the Democratic nomination as the party's presidential candidate. The organizational glitches, the money problems, the trek through interminable primaries and caucuses . . . all, all stretched ahead.

HAL YEAGER, THE ALABAMA JOURNAL/MONTGOMERY ADVERTISER

Although considered a long shot, the Rev. Jesse Jackson greets enthusiastic supporters on the campus of Alabama State University (right)

Profile of Sen. Gary Hart was recorded (right) late in the evening during an Iowa fund-raising appearance shortly before the Coloradoan announced his candidacy. Aspirant George McGovern (far right) is ignored by the family Yorky during a party in swanky condo on Chicago's Gold Coast.

DAVID L. CORNWELL, ROCKY MOUNTAIN NEWS, (DENVER COLO.)

DOM NAJOLIA, CHICAGO (ILL.) SUN-TIMES

ROBERT KOZLOFF, ASSOCIATED PRESS

Former Vice President Walter Mondale (above) makes point as he addresses the Democratic National Committee in Detroit, Mich.

Sen. John Glenn and wife Annie turn to acknowledge well-wishers in New Concord, Ohio (below).

DAVID I. ANDERSEN, THE PLAIN DEALER (CLEVELAND, OHIO)

OPPOSITE PAGE: In August, space
shuttle Challenger's third mission was
delayed by an electrical storm. Once
off, it carried into space the first U.S.
black astronaut: Air Force Lt. Col.
Guion Bluford.

An Air Canada 767 made a forced
landing on a drag strip at Gimli,
Manitoba, after both engines ran out
of fuel. There were no serious
injuries. Adds Photographer Wayne
Glowacki, "The circuit track racing
nearby carried on as scheduled."

WAYNE GLOWACKI, WINNIPEG (MAN.) FREE PRESS

In Nuevo Laredo, Mexico, two
officers talk to an Iranian-American
hijacker in an eventually successful
effort to effect the release of 21
hostages from a Rio Airways plane.
The hijacker was taken by another
plane to Mexico City and arrested.
Photographer Juan M. Garcia, in the
area on another story, says he
talked his way "past Mexico's army,
city police and airport police to
cover the story."

JUAN M. GARCIA, THE DALLAS (TEXAS) MORNING NEWS

It looks like the skeleton of a
beached whale: The burned-out shell
of a B-52G Superfortress which
exploded and burned on a runway at
Grand Forks, N.D., Air Force Base.
Five airmen died. Photographer
Jackie Lorentz says news teams
were allowed in, but not close.

JACKIE LORENTZ, GRAND FORKS (N.D.) HERALD

BILL THORUP, NASHVILLE (TENN.) BANNER

Above, at least one motorist was able to sit down and relax when traffic piled up on I-24 near Nashville, Tenn., as workmen dynamited rock for a new roadway. Left, neither rain, cold, nor flooding will stop one man from getting to his home in a San Jose, Calif., mobile home park. Opposite page: Police officer George Steen makes an editorial comment of sorts, as he handles a traffic pile-up during 100-degree heat in Fort Worth, Texas.

LEFT, MICHAEL J. BRYANT, SAN JOSE (CALIF.) MERCURY NEWS

OPPOSITE PAGE: PAUL F. MOSELEY, FORT WORTH (TEXAS) STAR-TELEGRAM

Above, a pair of two-mile long columns of motorcycles snakes through downtown Daytona Beach, Fla., during an impromptu parade to Daytona International Speedway.

Right, police officers on motorcycles and in squad cars lead a funeral procession in Marietta, Ga., for an officer who was killed when his car was struck by a driver subsequently charged with vehicular homicide.

Above, the morning after a section of the I-95 bridge over the Mianus River in Greenwich, Conn., simply dropped out. Three persons died, three were injured.

Below, pedestrians pull themselves up by ropes after El Salvadoran leftist guerrillas blew down the Urbina Bridge. The act cut the main highway between San Miguel and the Honduran border.

JOHN A. McDONNELL, THE MIDDLESEX NEWS, FRAMINGHAM, MASS.

Above, Massachusetts State troopers escort the casket of slain comrade John Hanna to funeral services. The trooper was gunned down during an apparently routine speeding stop.

The year 1983 erupted in great splashes of volcanic activity as pressures beneath the earth reawakened craters like Sicily's Mt. Etna (right) and Kilauea in Hawaii. Etna produced a 10-mph river of lava that carried along house-sized boulders and devastated more than 1,000 acres.

FIRST PLACE, MAGAZINE PICTORIAL, FERDINANDO SCIANNA, MAGNUM FOR LIFE

Rita Lavelle (above), deputy chief of the troubled Environmental Protection Agency, swore she didn't do anything wrong in failing to clean up toxic waste. A jury convicted her of perjury.

Sally Ride (right), first American woman in space, regretted ''that society isn't to the point yet where the country could just send up a woman astronaut and nobody would think twice about it.''

REZA-SIPA PRESS FOR TIME

TERRY ASHE, TIME

Yasser Arafat (above) at bay in Tripoli, where he came under attack from Palestine Liberation Organization rebels. At left, a long-faced moment in the public life of House Speaker Tip O'Neill.

Two images were combined to illustrate a story on alcoholism. It was published to coincide with the heavy drinking that occurs during the Christmas-New Year season.

SECOND PLACE, NEWSPAPER EDITORIAL ILLUSTRATION, JIM MENDENHALL, SAN JOSE (CALIF.) MERCURY NEWS

Picture above illustrated a story on what one deals with when building a house do-it-yourself. Hands belong to George Wedding, former Newspaper Photographer of the Year.

When the Dallas Times Herald's Westward Magazine needed an illustration for a story dealing with executions (below), Photographer Doug Milner volunteered as Photographer Michael Wirtz's model.

THIRD PLACE, NEWSPAPER EDITORIAL ILLUSTRATION, MICHAEL S. WIRTZ, DALLAS (TEXAS) TIMES HERALD

Fall fashions featured saturated color in Miami (above), furs in Philadelphia (right), and chains in Chicago (opposite page).

102

Photographer Michael J. Bryant worked hard to graft a zipper onto a potato.

Above, "Colby" the mouse (cost, $1.08) had its tail taped to a board to insure cooperation. Assignment complete, Colby joined Photographer Alan Berner's family. Photographer Marna Clarke got by with simpler props (below) in her assignment to make a photograph of hot peppers.

In his first time around with artichokes (above), Photographer Don Kohlbauer found backlighting helped with both texture and color.

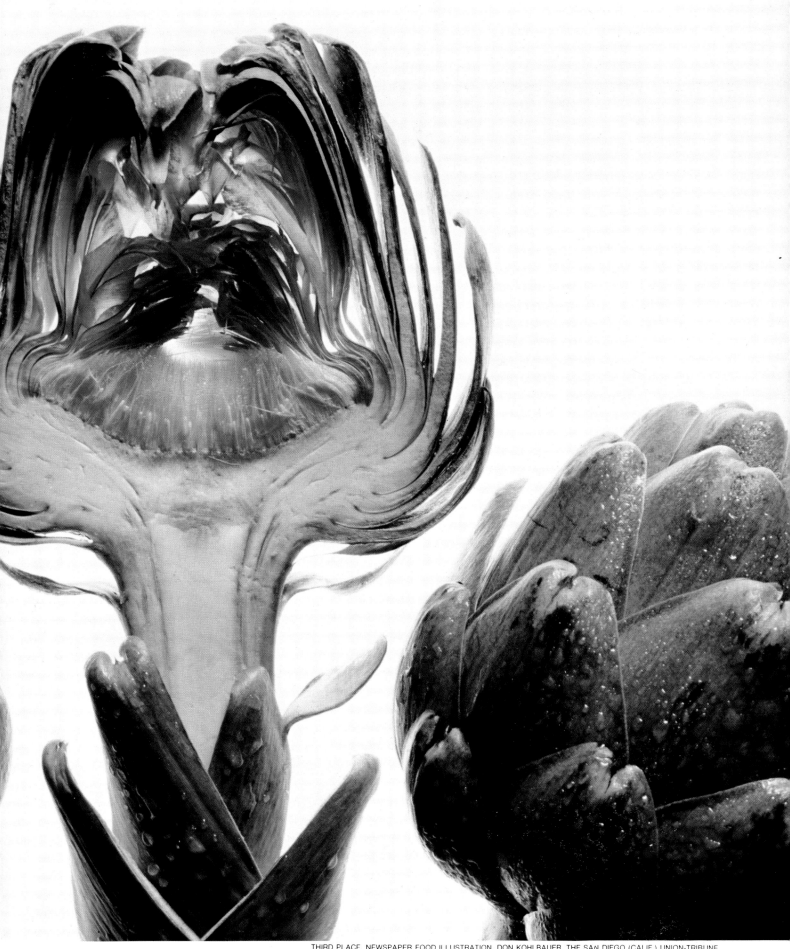

THIRD PLACE, NEWSPAPER FOOD ILLUSTRATION. DON KOHLBAUER, THE SAN DIEGO (CALIF.) UNION-TRIBUNE

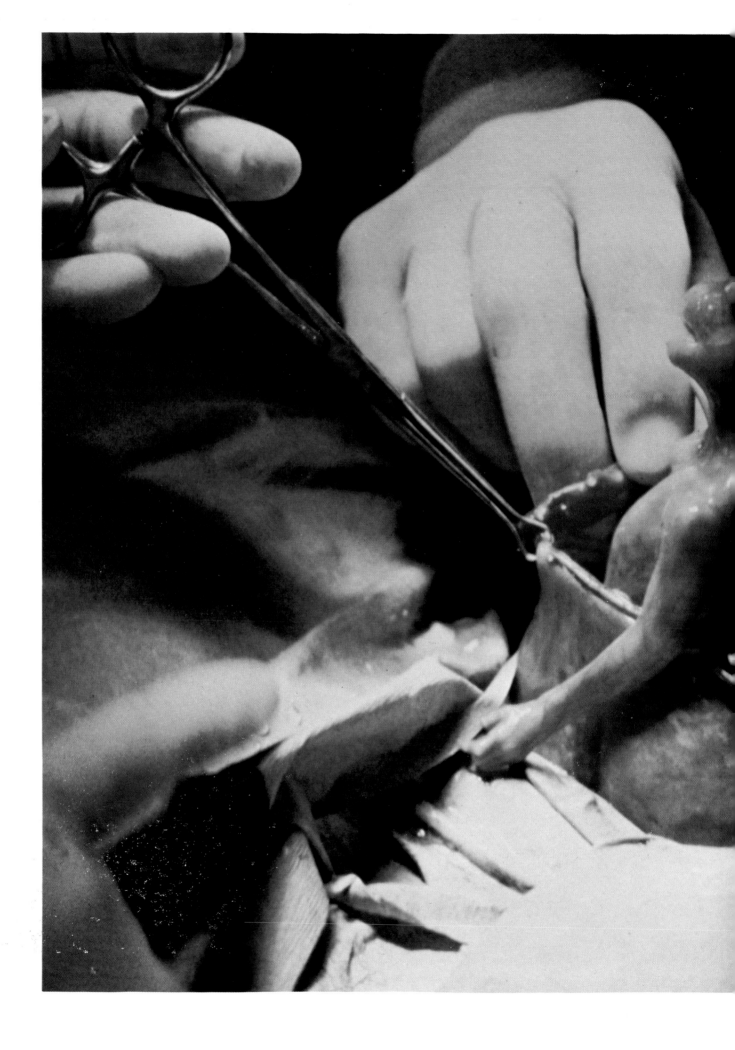

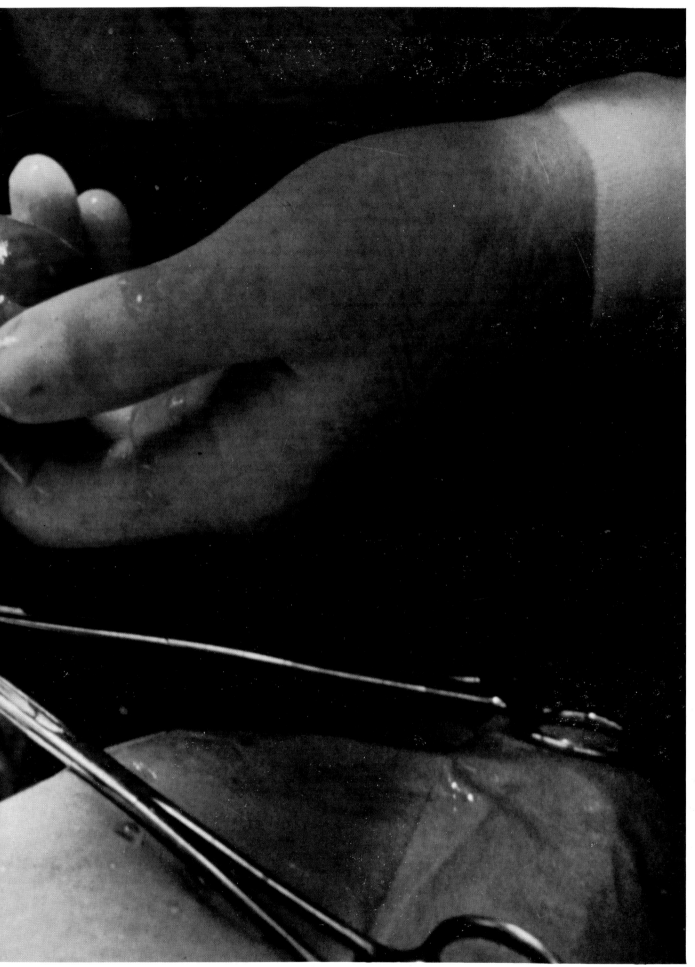

This 98-day old monkey fetus spent 10 minutes halfway out of the uterus during brain surgery. The experiment suggests that human fetuses might be similarly treated. Photograph is from "The Unborn Patient," a feature story showing radical new methods of treating the fetus.

MARI A. SCHAEFER, TUCSON (ARIZ.) CITIZEN

Early morning inspection proves too demanding for one Nicaraguan soldier (above). Photographer Mari A. Schaefer recorded his lapse during an awards ceremony at a military base in Chimaltenango. "Just made the soldier seem a little more human," she says.

Moslem woman in southern Beirut (below) stands in front of a bullet-torn wall of her home after the fighting has passed.

MAGAZINE PHOTOGRAPHER OF THE YEAR JAMES NACHTWEY, BLACK STAR FOR TIME

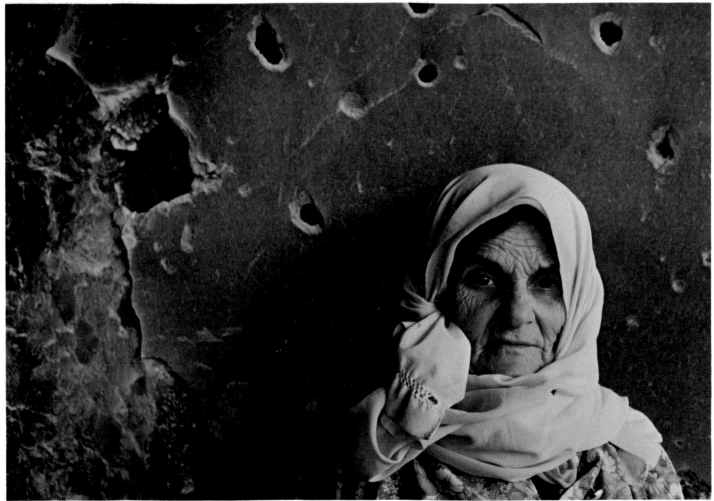

As more than a million exultant Poles cheer his entrance,
Pope John Paul II takes a flower-bordered route into
Warsaw's Tenth Anniversary Stadium in June. The picture
was part of a special section the Free Press printed to
report the Pope's visit. Photographer Tony Spina also
covered the Pope's visit to Poland in 1979.

HONORABLE MENTION, MAGAZINE FEATURE, JAMES L. AMOS, NATIONAL GEOGRAPHIC

Above, retracing the life and times of Martin Luther for the 500th anniversary of the theologian's birth, Photographer James Amos records a ritual performed by the faithful, who are following Luther's example. When he visited Rome in 1510, Luther ascended on his knees the Sacred Stairs near the Basilica of St. John Lateran, an obeisance that released a soul from purgatory.

Opposite page: Holy grottoes of Cappadocia once housed the largest community of monks in Asia Minor. From here missionaries spread the Christian faith as far as Ethiopia. Dwelling spaces for 30,000 were carved from the soft volcanic pinnacles between 4th and 14th centuries.

HONORABLE MENTION, MAGAZINE PICTORIAL, JAMES L. STANFIELD, NATIONAL GEOGRAPH

RICHARD E. KOZAK, THE JOURNAL (LORAIN, OHIO)

CONTRASTS IN CONTROL: Coast Guard cutter in the harbor at Lorain, Ohio (above), disrupts a flock of birds. Photographer Richard E. Kozak liked the situation because it permitted "no control of any of the elements of the photograph." In contrast (left), a study in complete control at The Citadel in Charleston, S.C., where cadets march across the courtyard of their barracks like toy soldiers.

THIRD PLACE, MAGAZINE FEATURE, ANNIE GRIFFITHS, NATIONAL GEOGRAPHIC

Study of Statue of Liberty (left) was part of The New York Times' assignment to capture the essence of the city. Photographer Fred R. Conrad used a 300-mm lens with an extender. But his advice to other shooters on working in New York: "If you don't get your picture on one corner, wait — or go to another corner."

Search for "wild art" in Chula Vista, Calif., resulted in study (right) of a marina, built since Photographer Vince Compagnone's last visit.

Photographer Mark R. Welsh knew the bleachers at Lawrence U. in Appleton, Wis., would make a good subject. But it took four months for the right situation to develop.

VINCE COMPAGNONE, LOS ANGELES (CALIF.) TIMES

MARK R. WELSH, THE POST-CRESCENT (APPLETON, WIS.)

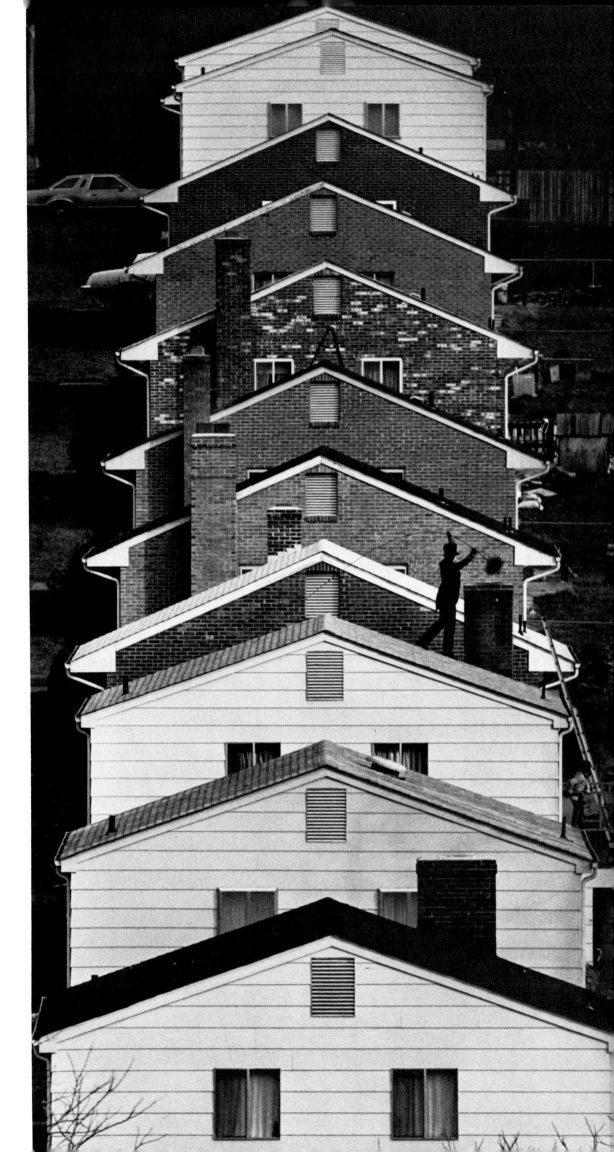

Left, Lila Dana has been answering other people's questions for four years in a San Jose, Calif. shopping center. Most frequently asked question: "Which way to the restrooms?"

Left, Photographer Talis Bergmanis flew over eastern Kansas looking for evidence of a winter storm's fury. Instead, he found a scenic view of an orchard.

Right, a long lens stacks up rooftops in Roanoke, Va., while a chimney sweep sweeps on, unknowing.

DON PETERSEN, ROANOKE (VA.) TIMES AND WORLD NEWS

BOB BLACK, CHICAGO (ILL.) SUN-TIMES

Assigned to make hot weather pictures on one of the steamiest days of the year, Photographer Bob Black wanted to avoid hydrants. But he decided the youngster creating patterns with this hydrant was just too good to pass up.

Photographer Bill Wade's reaction to a hot weather assignment was to make a photograph of a boy atop a falls on the Cuyahoga River in Kent, Ohio. Wade figured his paper would get adverse reader reaction. He was right.

BILL WADE, AKRON (OHIO) BEACON JOURNAL

Peter Allen is an Australian performer/choreographer who brought his stage show to The Pantages in Hollywood. Photographer Paul Chinn got off four frames before Allen reached the top of a mirrored staircase.

An amateur photographer focuses on dancers at San Diego's Organ Pavilion. Photographer James Skovmand decided the shooter was a better subject than the dancers.

Basque shepherd Benito Olea.

THIRD PLACE, NEWSPAPER FEATURE PICTURE STORY, JIMI LOTT, SPOKANE (WASH.) REVIEW AND CHRONICLE, ALL PHOTOS PPS. 120-123.

The Basque shepherd —

A vanishing breed

The Basque shepherd is an endangered species. Sheep owners of the American West have always considered Basques to be the ultimate shepherds. But as the sheep industry declines, and as the improving political situation in Spain makes emigration less attractive, the colorful Basques are rapidly disappearing from the remote rangelands of the West.

Most Basque shepherds are found in the high desert country of southern Idaho. Each encampment is a two-man operation: the shepherd, who spends his time out with his dogs watching the sheep; and the camp tender, who cooks, packs and moves the domed wagon that is their home.

It's a lonely way of life that's dying along with the sheep industry; there are only 150 Basque shepherds left in America.

The two-man team lives year-round in a small wagon of ancient design.

During precious leisure time, Juan Ercila reads a Spanish newspaper inside his cramped home on wheels.

The Basques

Sheep tender Juan Ercila's days are spent with two or three well-trained dogs and a thousand head of sheep.

Camp tender Gregario Ocamica checks the whereabouts of his partner.

Sheep tend to avoid humans — except for the sheep tender.

Camp tender Manuel Arteaga displays a loaf of his basketball-sized bread, cooked in an iron pot.

Normal pursuits are overshadowed by the development of offshore oil in California. Plant (below) purifies toxic gases brought from offshore sites. Says Photographer Michael J. Bryant: "Big bucks and big principles are at stake in a question facing California's future."

Robert Lee Yarbrough's shopping cartload of cans (above) was so long Photographer Kevin J. Manning couldn't get it all into his viewfinder.

Those are tears of joy (right), shed by a woman who waited more than 40 years to be baptized in the Ohio River at Louisville.

It was a pick-'em-yourself strawberry patch (below), but this youngster is more interested in hide 'n seek.

Above, this is a normal load for Raymond Baez. Each box contains foam plastic hats and weighs about five pounds. Baez moves each load a block and a half from a warehouse to an office building in downtown Hartford, Conn. "Once he balances the load on the hand truck," says Photographer Paul Miller, "his main worry is the wind."

Left, trucker Frank Keichline fights a losing battle with a load of cardboard boxes. His conclusion: "That's what you get for being too greedy."

Right, this contestant obviously didn't win a mud run for four-wheel vehicles in Ithaca, N.Y.

Below, wrestler Andy Ciambrone of Pope John Paul II High School in Boca Raton, Fla., had been listening to a running commentary from his coach on how to win his match. Finally, Andy responds.

JOHN METZGER, THE ITHACA (N.Y.) JOURNAL

DAVID MURRAY, JR., NEWS AND SUN-SENTINEL CO. (FORT LAUDERDALE, FLA.)

Horn players apparently exert a powerful photographic fascination. That's a trio of buglers (above), rehearsing for competition in Denver. Lower left, half-time action during a football game in Rhode Island. Lower right, a tuba player deals with frozen valves during a Merry Tuba Christmas Concert in Cleveland.

Beach Boys (above) rolled through the nation on the crest of a wave of nostalgia. This is a performance at the Mid-State Fair in San Luis Obispo, Calif.

Temperatures on the astro-turf topped 100 degrees when 60,000 people jammed the Cotton Bowl Stadium (below) in Dallas, Texas, for the annual Texxas Jam. Fire hoses are used to cool them down.

Leonard Faulkner, one of the last coopers in Louisville.

Author Tom Wolfe meets the press in the white suit that has become his trademark.

George Richard, 80, lives in a Seattle hotel used as a home for indigent men.

Jack Zarko's expression tells it all as he takes a break from playing the Easter Bunny in a Seattle doughnut shop, where he handed out samples to the kiddies.

THIRD PLACE, MAGAZINE PORTRAIT/PERSONALITY, WILLIAM COUPON, GEO

FIRST PLACE, MAGAZINE PORTRAIT/PERSONALITY, MICHAEL O'NEILL, LIFE

Arthur C. Clarke, author of "2001: A Space Odyssey," and 50 other books.

Larry King, most popular of the late-night radio talk show hosts.

Below: Jim Morris, 69, and Bill Weeb, 75, have lived together on the streets of Des Moines, Iowa, for 14 years. Says Photographer Rick Rickman, "They are the Butch and Sundance of the downtown transients."

HONORABLE MENTION, NEWSPAPER FEATURE PICTURE STORY, RICK RICKMAN, THE DES MOINES (IOWA) REGISTER

CRAMER GALLIMORE, FAYETTEVILLE (N.C.) OBSERVER-TIMES

HIRED HANDS: John Sanka (above), is one of three employees at the 40-year-old Bowens Island Seafood near Charleston, S.C., where customers have provided the interior decoration. At right is 16-year-old Paul Fortin, a summer worker on a Connecticut tobacco farm.

RIGHT, PAULA BRONSTEIN, NEW HAVEN (CONN.) REGISTER/JOURNAL

KEN AKERS, ARIZONA REPUBLIC (PHOENIX)

When Frank Sinatra stuck out his tongue (above), it was aimed at his wife, Barbara, during a benefit performance at Arizona State University in Tempe — just for fun. And when house painter Joe Markado stuck out his tongue (right), it was aimed at Photographer Howard Lipin — just for fun.

HOWARD LIPIN, ORANGE COAST DAILY PILOT (COSTA MESA, CALIF.)

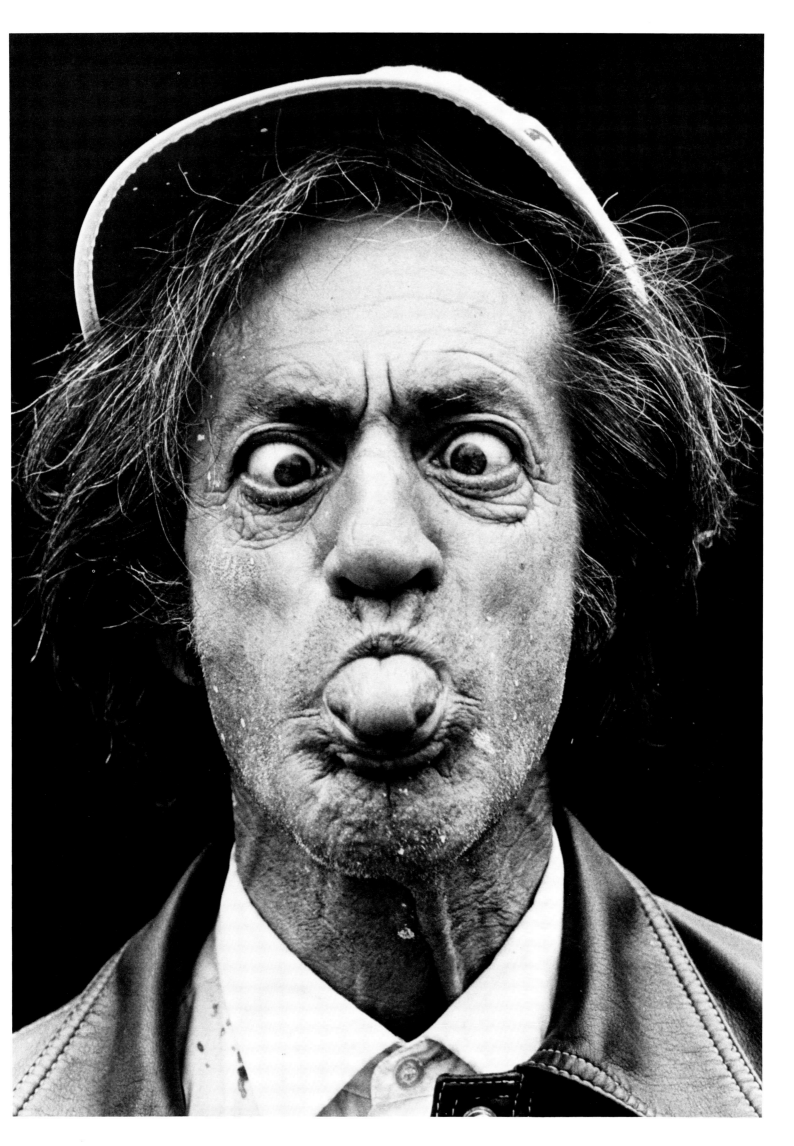

MARA A. LAVITT, THE NEW HAVEN (CONN.) REGISTER/JOURNAL COURIER

Comedian Eddie Murphy (above) offended some people in a sold-out crowd at an outdoor theater in Connecticut. Lower left, Genie Francis, who plays Laura on the TV soap, "General Hospital," didn't offend anyone in a personal appearance in Atlantic City. Lower right, Bette Midler knocked 'em out in Philadelphia with a scathing imitation of Jane Fonda working out.

APRIL SAUL, THE PHILADELPHIA (PA.) INQUIRER

APRIL SAUL

FRED BLOCHER, THE KANSAS CITY (MO.) TIMES

Operatic superstar Luciano Pavarotti mugs for photographers at a press conference in Kansas City, Mo.

DEBORA ROBINSON, FREELANCE FOR THE LOS ANGELES (CALIF.) TIMES

Rock superstar Boy George of the band, "Culture Club," sings for a sold-out crowd at the Pacific Amphitheater in Los Angeles.

For Janice Sterling in Norfolk, Va., bingo is not a game, it's a way of life. The question: Did she win this time?

JOHN LONG, THE HARTFORD (CONN.) COURANT

Photographer John Long figured it was just another 100th birthday anniversary. Then he met Eva Allen, former political activist now rationed to one cigarette a day. Concludes Long: "Sometimes you get lucky."

Sarah Biscardi looks more grandmotherly than amphibious (right). But the 57-year-old woman has been a lifeguard at the same pool in Hallandale, Fla., for 20 years. She's put on weight, but still passes all the lifesaving tests — and the kids love her.

Below, Francis Curcio, in a wheelchair, enters U.S. District Court in Hartford, Conn., to face charges of loan-sharking.

MARK EDELSON, THE SUN-TATTLER (HOLLYWOOD, FLA.)

ANACLETO RAPPING, THE HARTFORD (CONN.) COURANT

HONORABLE MENTION, NEWSPAPER GENERAL NEWS, JIM DAMASKE FOR THE CLEARWATER (FLA.) SUN

A 20-year-old exotic dancer (above) shows Judge David A. Demers that her bikini briefs are too large to expose what Clearwater undercover police say she exposed while performing at a nightclub. The case was dismissed.

An Ohio University professor (below) went to a Halloween block party in Athens, Ohio dressed (or undressed) as an absent-minded professor. He was arrested for disorderly conduct and mugged.

MARK KELLEY. JUNEAU EMPIRE/OHIO UNIVERSITY (ATHENS, OHIO)

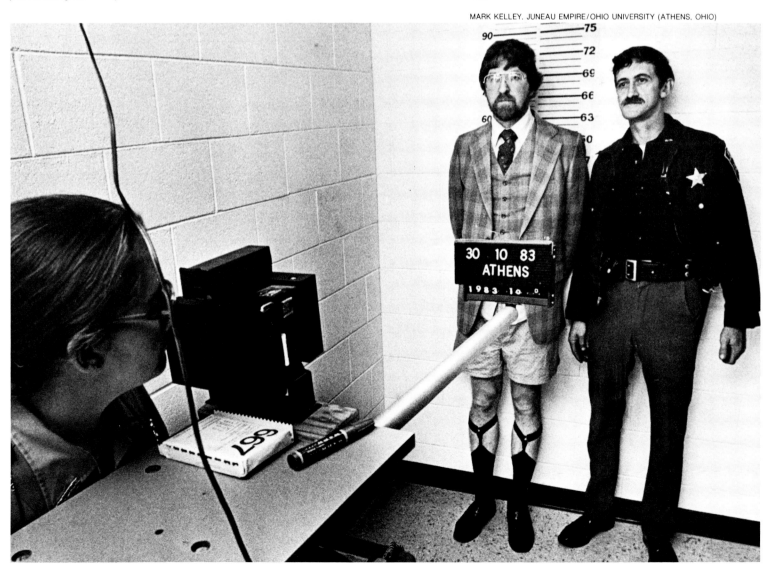

DAVID LASSMAN, SYRACUSE (N.Y.) NEWSPAPERS

JOHN KEATING, ST. LOUIS (MO.) POST-DISPATCH

When a gas explosion leveled a furniture store in Nedrow, N.Y., volunteer firefighter Barbara Findeisen's expression (above) spoke volumes. For another story-telling expression, how about the one on the face of a female customer (right) during a male stripper's performance at a St. Louis, Mo., night club?

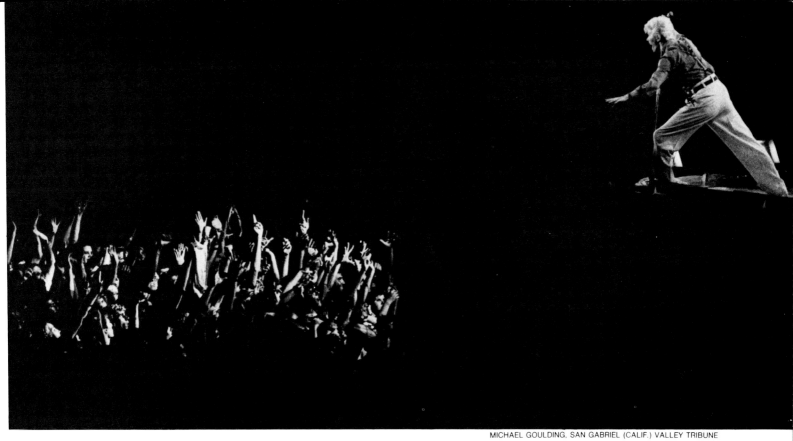

Above, Rock superstar David Bowie gets audience reaction during a concert appearance at the Anaheim, Calif., Stadium. Below, ballet superstar Mikhail Baryshnikov practices a dance routine in Minneapolis, Minn.

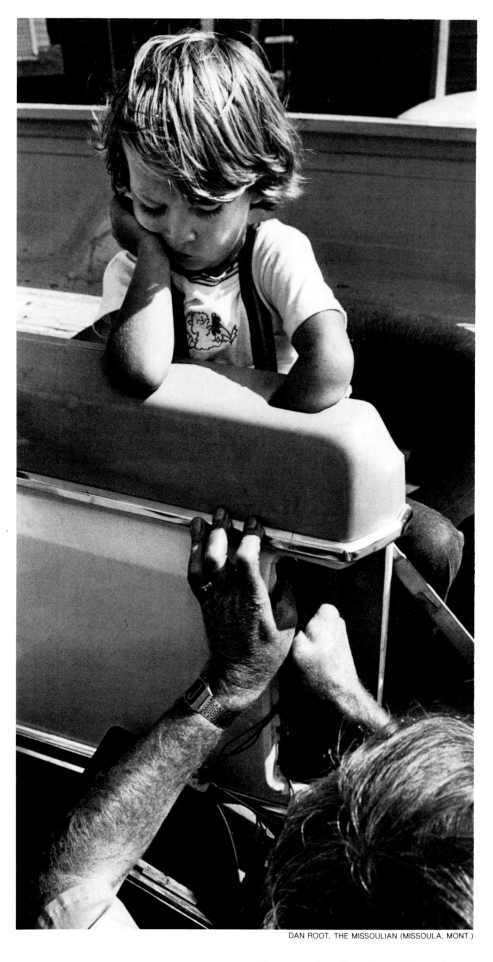

Photographer Dan Root followed
sirens from one assignment to find a
youngster with a problem. The boy
said he'd been hunting for bugs.

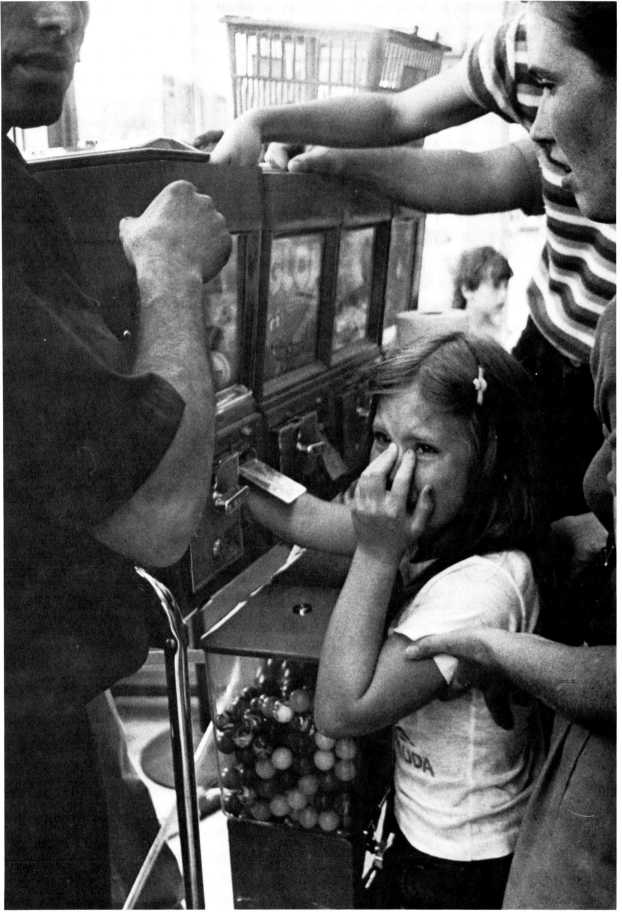

JIM MAHONEY, THE BOSTON (MASS.) HERALD

Lure of gumballs trapped this 7-year-old. Fireman unsuccessfully tried soap, vegetable oil, lubricating grease. Final, working solution: Break glass.

Overleaf: School girls walking between classes at the St. James Catholic School are caught in an updraft during one of San Francisco's winter storms.

OVERLEAF: NEWSPAPER PHOTOGRAPHER OF THE YEAR
STEVE RINGMAN, SAN FRANCISCO (CALIF.) CHRONICLE

MILAN CHUCKOVICH, THE IDAHO STATESMAN (BOISE, IDAHO)

Six-year-old Amy Wilson (above) was among 350 persons who participated in "Jazzerthon '83" at Boise State University. Purpose: to raise money for the Idaho Special Olympics.

Six-year-old Brian Fitzgerald, a policeman's son (below), gives the once-over to a rank of Explorer Scouts at a memorial service in Miami for policeman killed in action.

BILL REINKE, THE MIAMI (FLA.) NEWS

KEN KERBS, BALTIMORE (MD.) NEWS AMERICAN

For these Baltimore youngsters (above), election day means no classes. So, while their mothers work as poll officials inside the school building, the kids work off energy on the school yard.

Photographer Janet Knott's assignment: cover a sailing race. But she spied a bunch of kids pushing a stalled school bus in a small Maine town (below), and took time to record scene.

JANET KNOTT, THE BOSTON (MASS.) GLOBE

If this hog looks contented, it should; it's a resident of a museum and nature center in Stamford, Conn., where animals fill a visual, not dietary, need. Other than that, confesses Photographer Dru Nadler, "There's not much I can say about a photo of a pig."

OPPOSITE PAGE: While the Arizona Daily Star usually covers no more than one bullfight a year in pictures, Photographer Joe Patronite traveled to Nogales, Mexico, on a slow Sunday. His photograph of a bull wanting out made Page One.

BURR LEWIS, GANNETT ROCHESTER (N.Y.) NEWSPAPERS

In search of Thanksgiving feature, Photographer Burr Lewis chanced on a tom using a farmer's stomach as a vantage point to keep an eye on his harem of hens.

DAVID COATES, THE ROME (N.Y.) SENTINEL

"Dolly" the pug and "Bird" the robin became friends after the dog's young master rescued the robin. "Bird" is free to go. Won't.

Photographer Al Podgorski
spotted this stray cat while
cruising for enterprise art.

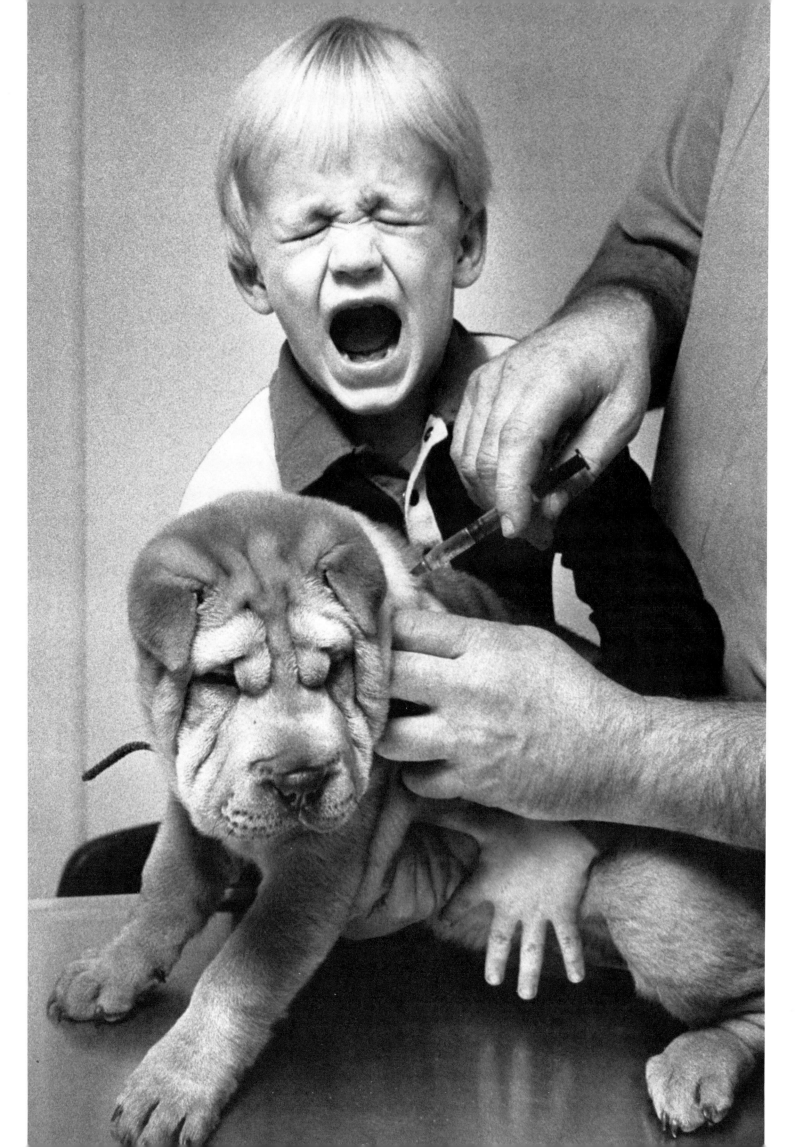

BRAD GRAVERSON, THE DAILY BREEZE (TORRANCE, CALIF.)

Above, Helena LeCount of Lawndale, Calif., swings her pit bull "Othello" in a game of tug of war intended to strengthen the dog's jaws.

Left, talk about empathy! 4-year-old Corey Scholar reacts to booster shot being given to his Chinese Shar-pei puppy in Reading, Pa.

LEFT, JANET KELLY, READING (PA.) EAGLE-TIMES

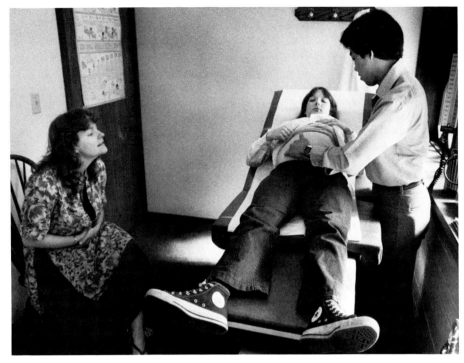

As soon as Jennifer learned she was pregnant, she had regular appointments to see her obstetrician. At times, Kate was as much a patient as Jennifer.

On a day off from her job as a technical editor at a computer firm, Jennifer visits a nearby beach.

Toby's mothers

They live in a world that thinks lesbians and children don't mix. But Kate started saving baby clothes at 15, and Jennifer could never imagine a life without kids. Once they found each other, though they knew it wouldn't be easy, they decided to go ahead with their dream.

The couple found a donor and artificially inseminated Jennifer. Nine months later, in July, their son was born.

Photographer Karen Borchers followed them from Jennifer's fourth month of pregnancy.

"In the past," explains Borchers, "stories I have seen dealing with lesbians have shown them in stereotypical roles ... It seemed reasonable to strike a balance and show another side of lesbian life, especially one where children were involved.

"We knew it was a controversial, sensitive subject, one that would upset a lot of people. But it also was an important, timely story that deserved to be published."

HONORABLE MENTION, CANON PHOTO ESSAYIST, KAREN T. BORCHERS, SAN JOSE (CALIF.) MERCURY NEWS, ALL PHOTOS PAGES 156-161

Toby's mothers

At a baby shower, friends give the mothers-to-be clothes, a baby carrier, and several stuffed bears.

Kate and Jennifer attend a birth class with heterosexual couples, practicing relaxation techniques.

Jennifer visits a spa, something she did as often as possible to get proper exercise.

Jennifer fixes lunch in the couple's kitchen. Do they fight? Says Kate, "We argue ... but don't scream."

The couple lives with three cats and an Irish setter in a one-bedroom mountain cabin.

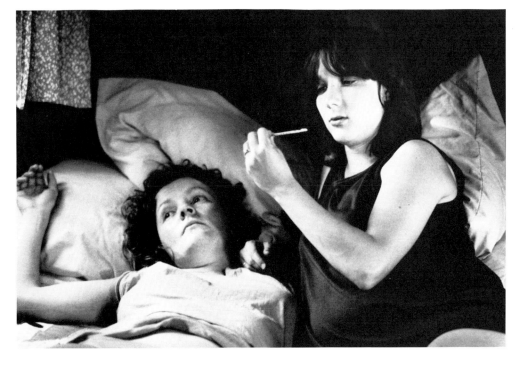

Jennifer takes Kate's temperature after she complained of an upset stomach and fever.

Above, Jennifer packs her bag with supplies in anticipation of the birth.

Left, friends and a coach give Jennifer support, help her to breathe.

Christopher David Tobias was born at 9 a.m. Below, Jennifer sips water.

Toby's mothers

At home, Toby gets sunshine on the porch while Kate gazes, entranced.

Jennifer gives Toby a late afternoon feeding.

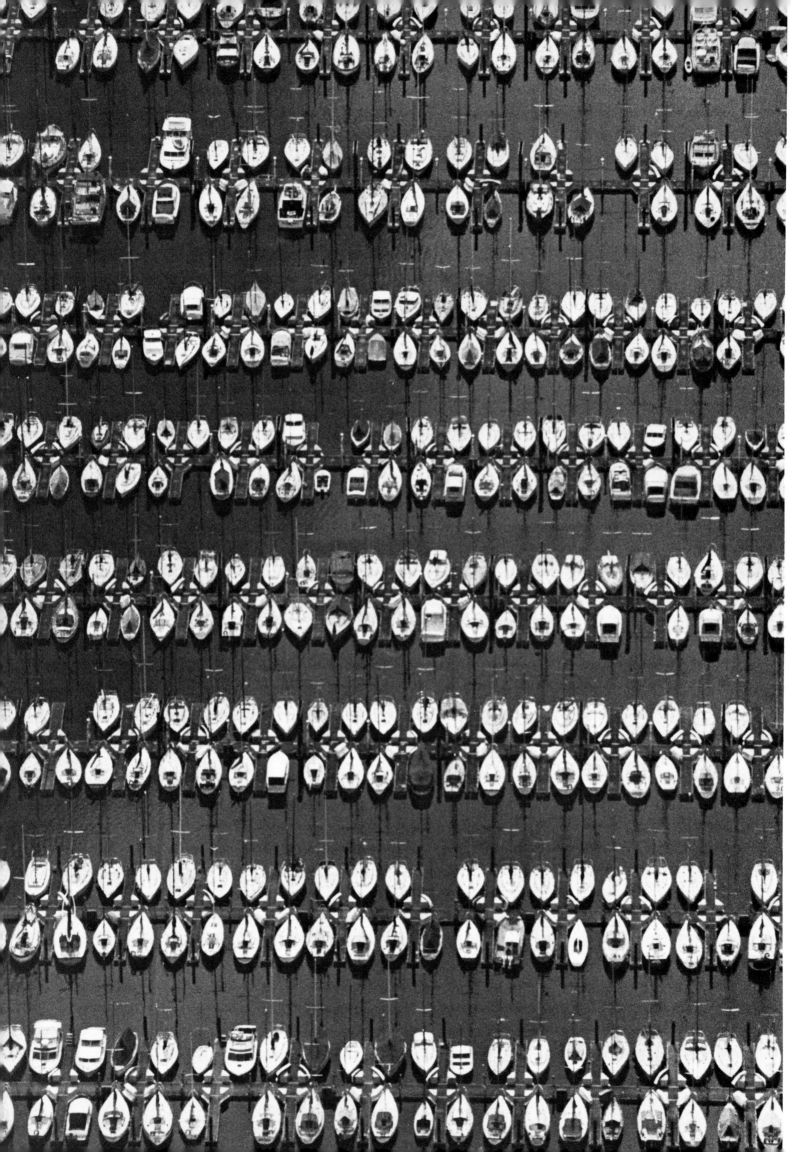

LEFT, GRANT M. HALLER, SEATTLE (WASH.) POST-INTELLIGENCER

C.W. McKEEN, SYRACUSE (N.Y.) HERALD-AMERICAN

Pattern of boats (left) moored in Shilshole Bay Marina, Seattle, Wash., was recorded as Photographer Grant M. Haller returned from another assignment.

Security people at plant in Syracuse, N.Y. (above), didn't want Photographer C.W. McKeen to make this picture. He did, anyhow. "The window washer loved it," reports McKeen.

Everyone shoots up at balloons — except Photographer Cathy Acherman. She rode in another balloon to make picture (below) during U.S. National Hot Air Balloon championships in Indianola, Iowa.

CATHY ACHERMAN, BARRINGTON (ILL.) COURIER-REVIEW

Overcrowding was such a problem in the county jail at Spokane, Wash. (right), that eight prisoners were placed in the same cell. Problems of Philadelphia, Pa., street people were doubly poignant during the Christmas season, which found one man (below) huddled over a street vent.

TOM GRALISH, THE PHILADELPHIA (PA.) INQUIRER

THIRD PLACE, NEWSPAPER PHOTOGRAPHER OF THE YEAR JOHN KAPLAN, THE SPOKANE (WASH.) SPOKESMAN-REVIEW

Sister Mary Gauvin had a ball catching beads during a Mardi Gras parade in New Orleans. But she didn't like the looks of Photographer Eliot Kamenitz, and gave a phony name.

A jubilant student (above) at Central Connecticut State University gives a normal response during graduation ceremonies in New Britain, Conn.

News teams converged on Bering Sea when members of the environmentalist organization Greenpeace were released by the Russians after detention for attempts to publicize Soviets' wrongful use of whale meat. Left, a Greenpeacer gives victory sign as lifeboat leaves a Russian vessel. Photographer Paul Brown's assessment: "A media circus."

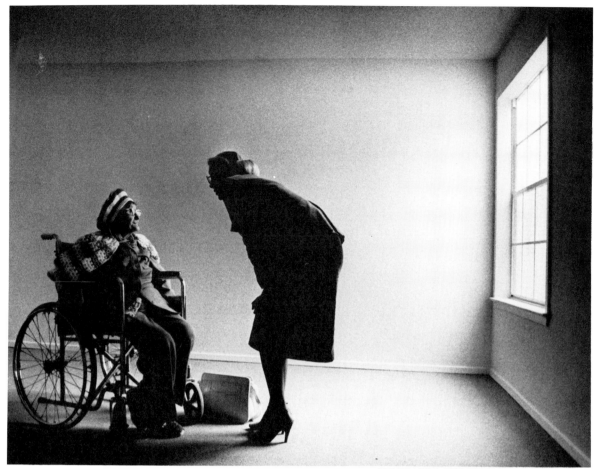

Above, Debbie Lietz, a Department of Human Resources case worker, gets Delia Ashcraft's opinion of her new apartment in an Arlington, Texas, group facility for people who don't need nursing care but who can't maintain their own homes.

Photographer Phil Skinner spotted trio (right) through his auto's rear view mirror in Highland Beach, Fla. A U-turn put him into shooting position.

KURT F. MUTCHLER, THE TIMES-PICAYUNE (NEW ORLEANS, LA.)

Lyle B. Smith (left), a World War II veteran, salutes a passing flag during a VFW parade. "He wasn't in the parade himself," says Photographer Kurt F. Mutchler, "but he really showed what everybody was parading about."

Below, young-at-heart couples dance in a Louisville park pavilion during a senior citizens' day.

THIRD PLACE, NEWSPAPER FEATURE, BARBARA MONTGOMERY, THE COURIER-JOURNAL, LOUISVILLE (KY.) TIMES

LARRY STEAGALL, YAKIMA (WASH.) HERALD-REPUBLIC

LANCE WYNN, GANNETT ROCHESTER (N.Y.) NEWSPAPERS

WILLIAM SNYDER, THE DALLAS (TEXAS) MORNING NEWS

CLOCKWISE FROM UPPER LEFT:
John Vauthiers, 60, spends his
summers in Liberty, Wash., mining
for gold; Gray Panthers founder
Maggie Kuhn, 78, at a press
conference in Rochester, N.Y.; and
Bill, a gentleman of the streets in
Dallas, Texas, who says he is a
schizophrenic.

Just like that, peripatetic entrepreneurs with inflatable jeans were on every (well, not *every)* vacant lot in the country. From top: A customer blends in with the display in Dallas, Texas; a wind- and salesman-blown lash-up in Jackson, Miss.; a cutoffs-clad dealer in Baltimore, Md.

HONORABLE MENTION, NEWSPAPER PORTRAIT/PERSONALITY, ANTHONY SUAU, THE DENVER (COLO.) POST

In Denver, high school punks posture in an alley.

Above, in San Jose, Calif., Stacy Pagter plays a hot fiddle, so hot it can make the boughs sway as if to the music.

Below: after a performance, puppeteer and puppet head for home.

NEWSPAPER PHOTOGRAPHER OF THE YEAR STEVE RINGMAN, SAN FRANCISCO (CALIF.) CHRONICLE

Every summer in San Francisco, the Gay Parade is opened by a group of lesbian women on motorcycles. The group of bikers is called "Dykes on Bikes."

SETH RESNICK, SYRACUSE (N.Y.) NEWSPAPERS

A front tire blowout ended 63-year-old Milt Sorenson's hopes for a triathlon win in Syracuse, N.Y.

Left, Vance Hubersberger of Beulah, Colo., soars over his wife, Shellie, while practicing his hotdog bicycling skills. He's the 1982 and '83 co-world record holder in the "bunny hop," in which the cyclist jumps his vehicle over a pole without benefit of a ramp. Hubersberger can jump his bike more than 41 inches.

LEFT, CURT CHANDLER, PUEBLO (ARIZ.) CHIEFTAIN

FRED R. CONRAD, THE NEW YORK TIMES

Big blasts of fireworks saluted the 100th anniversary of New York City's Brooklyn Bridge in May (above), and Fourth of July observances in Washington, D.C. (below, left), where the National Symphony Orchestra performs at the Capitol, and in Los Angeles, Calif. (below, right), where the University of Southern California's symphony plays at the Hollywood Bowl.

JULIA GAINES, THE WASHINGTON (D.C.) TIMES

JAVIER MENDOZA, LOS ANGELES (CALIF.) HERALD EXAMINER

Biggest blizzard ever to hit South Jersey left more than enough snow for a gallant lover to stomp out a Valentine's Day sentiment (above). And in Chicago (below), a dusting of fresh snow gives a different look to an Amtrak railroad yard.

Human hand belongs to Steve Hill, a member of the First Congregational Church of Windham Center, Conn. He's in the process of repairing the church's clock, which had been broken for years.

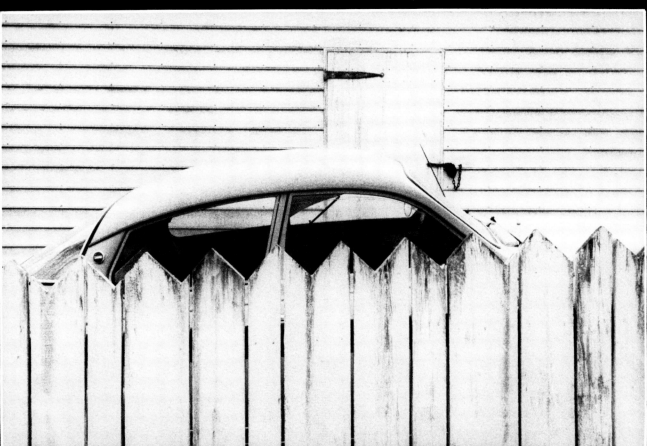

Photographer Gary Gunderson made this photograph in Colonial Williamsburg, didn't print the film until eight

Mist rose from a pond to shroud hundreds of ducks during
a week-long deep freeze in Denver, Colo.

Cedar waxwings, 47 strong, assemble for a group portrait,
the first film exposed by Photographer Joe Abell after
hospitalization for a near-fatal asthma attack.

At left, a pair of stubborn anglers refuses to remove lines from Lake Michigan as a school of swimmers passes by on the first leg of a triathalon meet. Says Photographer Chris Walker, "One fisherman complained to another, 'Every week it's something different!'"

At right, an old priest walks a familiar route through St. Peter's Square in Rome to his accustomed place of prayer.

Photographer Stephen D. Dunn was assigned to cover a
100-craft Hobie Cat race. It was cancelled: thick fog, no
wind. When these two quit playing they were towed in.

Security guard at the Baltimore Art
Museum takes advantage of light
and warmth during a break.

Left, trying for a spring weather photograph, Photographer Bern Ketchum found a storm cell over a wheat field. He made a dozen exposures as the lightning kept striking, and quit when it got too close.

Below, near Peacham, Vt., Lawrence Woodward adjusts the harness on his team during spring plowing.

FIRST PLACE, NEWSPAPER PICTORIAL, BERN KETCHUM, TOPEKA (KAN.) CAPITAL-JOURNAL

THIRD PLACE, MAGAZINE PICTORIAL, RICHARD W. BROWN, BLAIR & KETCHUM'S COUNTRY JOURNAL (MANCHESTER CENTER, VT.)

Members of the Gandhi Memorial International Foundation march across the sands of Santa Monica Beach to begin an observance of Gandhi Week with a peace vigil.

OVERLEAF: Japanese drummers of the KODO group beat on a 500-pound drum, an o-daiko, on a beach on the remote island of Sado, where they live a spartan lifestyle, very close to the elements. They often practice outdoors.

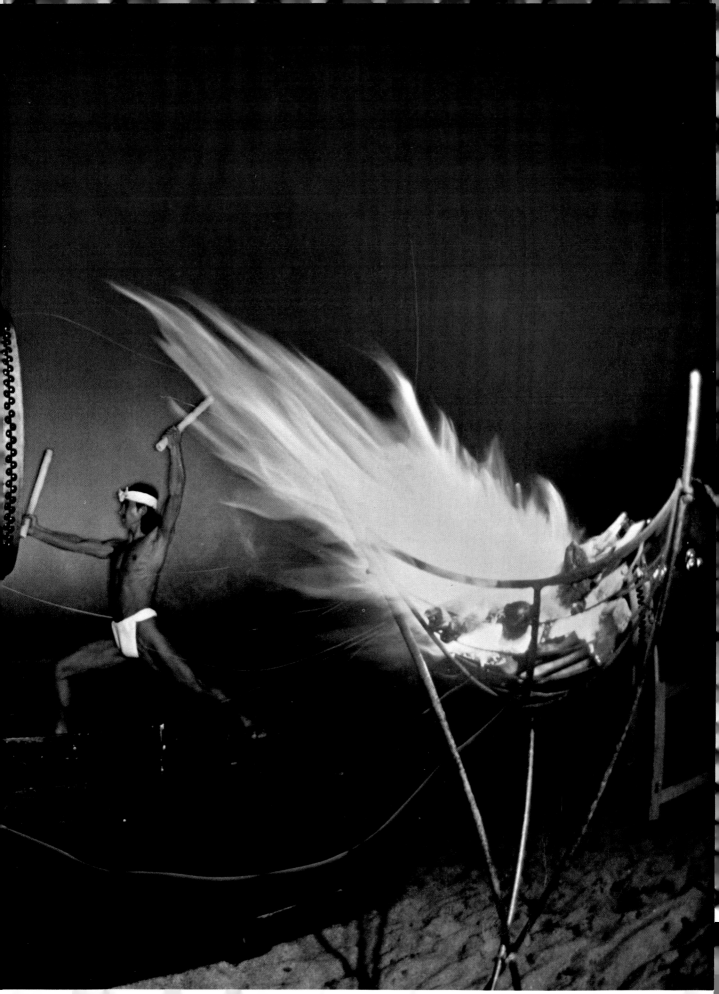

Fun 'n games

Pros and amateurs, big leagues and bush, games were nothing to play with in 1983. They won 'em and they lost 'em, and the news photographer was there to record it.

The Baltimore Orioles took the Series in five. The L.A. Raiders owned Super Bowl XVIII; and Nebraska's Cornhuskers had it all their way in college football — until they met Miami.

George Brett had all that crazy business about pine tar on his bat — and the Liberty lost to Australia II and the America's Cup went down under after 132 years.

That heavyweight legend, Jack Dempsey, died at age 87. And the Islanders took their fourth consecutive Stanley Cup. The Tom Watsons and John McEnroes and the Roberto Durans were hard at it . . . all grist for the photojournalists' mill.

The Baltimore Orioles' jubilant pitcher, Tippy Martinez (right), climbs aboard catcher Rick Dempsey as the Orioles post a 10th-inning win over the Chicago White Sox during fourth game of the American League championship series. Baltimore then went on to clinch a World Series berth, and beat the Philadelphia Phillies for all the marbles.

Opposite page: Phillies' pitcher Al Holland and catcher Mike Schmidt react after their team wraps up the National League championship by beating the Los Angeles Dodgers.

Left, University of Maryland fans knock down a goalpost after Maryland defeated North Carolina, 28-26. Right, Woody Bennett scores a touchdown that contributes to a 14-0 victory over the New York Jets.

LEFT, HONORABLE MENTION, MAGAZINE SPORTS, GEORGE TIEDEMANN, CONTRACT FOR SPORTS ILLUSTRATED

THIRD PLACE, MAGAZINE SPORTS, GEORGE TIEDEMANN, CONTRACT FOR SPORTS ILLUSTRATED

THIRD PLACE, NEWSPAPER PICTORIAL, TOM BURTON, THE ORLANDO (FLA.) SENTINEL

If — as Sportswriter Red Smith is supposed to have said — sports are games played by little boys, this pair qualifies. It's an elementary school playground in Orlando, Fla.

FIRST PLACE, NEWSPAPER SPORTS FEATURE, PAUL F. MOSELEY, FORT WORTH (TEX.) STAR-TELEGRAM

Teammates (above) carry home run hitter David Springer off the field after Carroll, Tex., High School team advances to the state semi-finals.

Washington Redskins' Alvin Garrett (below) gets physical credit for winning touchdown against the Dallas Cowboys. Win put the Redskins into the Super Bowl.

TOMMY PRICE, VIRGINIAN PILOT/LEDGER STAR (NORFOLK, VA.)

They may not have originated the "High Five" (left), but members of the Mississippi Gulf Coast Junior College baseball team performed it when they won a college district championship.

Below left, a pumped-up Terry Tyler gives his solo version of the High Five as the Detroit Pistons post a last-minute win over the Milwaukee Bucks.

Below right, the Washington Redskins "Fun Bunch" not only originated High Five, they perfected it. Here they go into their routine during a game against Minnesota. The NFL has deemed such displays will draw a five-yard penalty.

DINAH ROGERS, THE SUN/THE DAILY HERALD (BILOXI, MISS.)

STEVE FECHT, UNITED PRESS INTERNATIONAL

GARY A. CAMERON, THE WASHINGTON (D.C.) POST

How sweet it is

Players on the bench for the University of Alabama at Huntsville cheer their comeback efforts as the Lady Chargers defeat Campbellsville (Ky.) College in the NAIA tournament.

St. John's Billy Goodwin celebrates after his team defeats Boston College in Madison Square Garden for the Big East championship.

JOE CRACHIOLA, THE MACOMB DAILY (MOUNT CLEMENS, MICH.)

KEITH MEYERS, THE NEW YORK TIMES

JOHN FILO, THE PHILADELPHIA (PA.) INQUIRER

Clockwise from left: New York Rangers pile up after scoring during an NHL playoff game against the Philadelphia Flyers. Detroit quarterback Eric Hipple embraces rookie receiver Jeff Chadwick after they teamed up for a touchdown pass against the Tampa Bay Buccaneers to clinch the NFC Central championship. Rod Dixon exults after he overtook Geoff Smith in the last mile to win the New York City Marathon, while Smith collapses in exhaustion.

FIRST, NEWSPAPER SPORTS ACTION, JIMI LOTT, SPOKANE (WASH.) REVIEW AND CHRONICLE

NCAA record holder Milt Ottey of Washington State University clears the bar during NCAA track and field meet in Houston, Texas. This time he didn't win.

In Fort Worth, Texas, Adrian Muehlstein clears the bar to win pole-vaulting event in a junior track meet for 12-and 13-year-olds.

In Kettering, Ohio, Chris Cultrice of East High School tries (but fails) to place in pole-vaulting event during a 10-team meet.

In Winston-Salem, N.C., Ricky McCaskill of Parkland High School clears the bar at the 6'6'' mark to win the high jump event in a regional meet.

Dan Quisenberry, relief pitcher for the Kansas City Royals, hoses down bleacher fans during a 98-degree heat wave.

In Boston's Fenway Park, Red Sox fans say goodbye to
Carl Yastrzemski, 44, who retired after 23 seasons.

The solitude and loneliness of his training regimen show as Wayne Boyd takes an early morning jog (below). Opposite page: Boyd works out daily in a gymnasium, developing muscles he'd forgotten he owned.

FIRST PLACE, NEWSPAPER SPORTS PICTURE STORY, RAYMOND GEHMAN, THE VIRGINIAN PILOT/LEDGER STAR (NORFOLK, VA.)

One more shot . . .

Nineteen years ago, when Wayne Boyd was 17 and a junior in high school, he advanced to the final trials for the U.S. Olympic wrestling team. He has traveled that road twice more, in 1968 and 1972.

Boyd is 36 now, divorced, father of two teenagers. His heart still pumps desire, and it points his head to Los Angeles, and the impossible dream of the 1984 Summer Olympics. One more shot, he says: give me one more shot.

Late in 1983, Boyd took a one-year leave of absence from his $30,000-a-year job to train full time. He has not wrestled in competition since 1977.

Boyd's an old man, for an Olympics wrestler. It just isn't done.

"The only way I'll know if I'm good enough is to try," he says. "I've got to know."

Boyd works on his moves with a member of the wrestling team at Old Dominion University, then tries to deal with the loss of a match.

Wrestler

Boyd was disheartened when he lost a match (above) in the Eastern Nationals. But he won four of his next five. Right, an exhausted Boyd takes the end of one workout lying down.

No grins

Members of the Walton High School girls' basketball team, number one seed in Georgia's state tournament, watch time run out in their bid for the title. Says Photographer John W. Rossino, "I got lucky; the girls didn't."

Body English tells the story of these girls from Rochester John Marshall High School as their unbeaten basketball season slips away at the Minnesota state tournament.

MARLIN LEVISON, MINNEAPOLIS (MINN.) STAR AND TRIBUNE

Depths of despair were touched by Burton Chalaire, player on the St. Bernard (La.) High School football team, during the last seconds of his team's 22nd straight defeat. But there's more, says Photographer Chuck Cook: "They went on to lose the rest of their games ... the streak now stands at 26."

CHUCK COOK, THE NEW ORLEANS (LA.) TIMES-PICAYUNE

JOHN ROSSINO, MARIETTA (GA.) DAILY JOURNAL

MARY SCHROEDER, DETROIT (MICH.) FREE PRESS

Detroit Lions players James Jones, Leonard Thompson, Mark Nichols and Gary Danielson react as kicker Eddie Murray misses a field goal with five seconds to go in their playoff game with San Francisco.

How few milli-seconds separated the shutters of two photographers who made these views of baseball action? Each was made during the first game of the American League playoffs in Baltimore, Md.: Baltimore's Al Bumbry high-slides into Chicago White Sox second baseman Julio Cruz in an attempt to break up a double play. Says Photographer Gary Cameron, "Most of us covering the championships and World Series thought it was one of the better photo opportunities." But neither Cameron nor Photographer Louis DeLuca could have known just how close they came to recording exactly the same slice of time.

BIRD IN THE HAND: Usually, baseball players are chasing loose dogs from the field. But in two instances the loose critters were parakeets. At left, Texas Ranger catcher Jim Sundberg uses whatever's at hand to try get the bird in Arlington Stadium. Below, St. Louis Cardinal Andy Van Slyke chases another elusive bird around right field during a game with the Chicago Cubs in Wrigley Field.

GERALD R. SCHUMANN, FREELANCE FOR UNITED PRESS INTERNATIONAL

JOHN SWART, ASSOCIATED PRESS

Amish youngster in Ohio is a study in coltish joy.
Photographer Eric Albrecht says she was "more interested
in the ball game than another stranger watching . . . "

High School pitcher in Colorado is a study in adolescent determination. Photographer David Denney says he saw this windup: "From that point on, the picture is a gift."

So close . . .

DAVID BINDER, ANCHORAGE (ALASKA) DAILY NEWS

Ruth Thoemke stoops and glares —
but the ball doesn't drop. She was
competing in the Alaska amateur
women's golf tournament.

BRIAN M. LaPETER, THE ISLAND PACKET (HILTON HEAD ISLAND, S.C.)

Betty Probasco reacts when her try
for a birdie failed. She was defending
champion in a senior women's
tourney on Hilton Head Island, S.C.

Texas Wesleyan's Danny Mijovic shows total dismay when he misses an 18th-hole putt that would have won NIAI title outright for his team.

Obviously, Darren Downey of Harrisonville, Mo., is not thinking kind thoughts. His missed putt came during a Junior PGA tournament.

HONORABLE MENTION, NEWSPAPER SPORTS ACTION, PHIL SKINNER, NEWS AND SUN-SENTINEL CO. (FORT LAUDERDALE, FLA.)

Above, Florida high school soccer produced frame full of action on a corner kick. Left below, Win Rijsbergen (No. 15) of the New York Cosmos, takes a head shot on the goal of Team America. Right below, head action in a Texas high school game.

JAMES FIEDLER, JR., THE WASHINGTON (D.C.) TIMES   JOE ABELL, SAN ANGELO (TEXAS) STANDARD-TIMES

Above, Jimmy Conners in a moment of self-criticism during the U.S. Open tennis tournament in September. He went on to win his second consecutive and fifth U.S. Open title. At left, during the same tourney, Bill Scanlon reacts to his upset victory over John McEnroe.

While Photographer Steve Koger thinks baseball is boring, he's willing to admit it has its moments (left above), as when Kevin Dale, third baseman for Hagerstown (Ind.) High School, muffs a fly ball.

Nothing was injured (right above) except pride when Chanute, Kan., shortstop Karl Krokstrom's glasses went one way and the ball another. Action came in a VFW League game. Chanute lost.

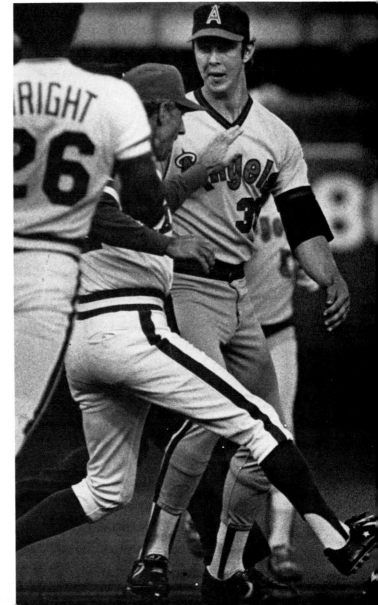

Somewhere in the middle of all those bodies (right) are the Texas Rangers' Wayne Tollefson and the California Angels' Bobby Grich, who ignited a free-for-all in the first inning of a game at the Rangers' Arlington Stadium. (Oh, yes — the Rangers won.)

High, hard one is delivered by New York Mets pitcher Mike Torrez. His target: Atlanta Braves pitcher Rick Camp. That's Mets first baseman Rick Camp in the middle.

This confrontation between California Angels Bobby Grich and Texas Rangers' Wayne Tolletson led to the melee shown below.

Standing tall (left) Oklahoma State's
LeRoy Combs and Raymond
Crenshaw respond to a fake by
Missouri guard Prince Bridges.
Action came during final game of the
Big Eight post season tournament in
Kansas City, Kan. Oklahoma State
upset Missouri, won the tournament.

Standing tall (right), Ralph
Sampson of the Virginia
Cavaliers dwarfs other players
in NCAA regional playoff game
against Boston College at
Ogden, Utah. Cavaliers won
this game, dropped the title
game to North Carolina State.
Sampson went to the pros with
the Houston Rockets.

JAMES GARCIA, THE DAILY JOURNAL (FERGUS FALLS, MINN.)

It was just another district tournament game in small-town Minnesota (above), pitting Barnesville against Pelican Rapids. But it provided classic stop action of a fast break. Left below, the Los Angeles Lakers' Magic Johnson reaches for the net after scoring against the Philadelphia 76ers in opening game of the NBA championship series in May. The Lakers lost. Right below, the University of Wisconsin's Faith Johnson is surrounded by all five of the Minnesota Gophers team as she drives in for a lay-up at Williams Arena in Minneapolis. The Badgers lost, however.

BRAD BOWER, FREELANCE FOR UNITED PRESS INTERNATIONAL

DAVID BREWSTER, MINNEAPOLIS (MINN.) STAR AND TRIBUNE

Gut-wrenching contact (right) as New York Jet Abdul Salaam slams into Ron Lee of the Miami Dolphins caused a fumble during the AFC championship in Miami. But the Dolphins went on to the Super Bowl. Below, UCLA running back Frank Cephous rises from the end zone to accolades from the sidelines. His late-game touchdown gave the Bruins a Rose Bowl-clinching win over the Washington Huskies, and the Bruins then went on to win the team's second straight Rose Bowl championship.

Right, Washington Redskin John Riggins goes up and over two Dallas Cowboys to score in the NFL National Conference title game in Washington, D.C. The Redskins won, then went on to beat the Miami Dolphins in the Super Bowl. Below, nothing is going right for Army in its traditional game against Navy. Now the annual game will be held in the Rose Bowl, where the Midshipmen sank the Cadets, 42-13, with plays like this pass deflection.

Gravy Bowl?

An informal tradition known as "The Turkey Bowl" brings out the Old Boys in Wilmington, Del., every Thanksgiving Day.

These are former football players at Brandywine High School, who get together on Thanksgiving to talk, touch, catch up with things and (just incidentally) to play some football.

Photographer Fred Comegys says he covered "the needy with their meals, but the paper ended up using a small layout on the football, which was a welcome change."

THIRD PLACE, NEWSPAPER SPORTS PICTURES STORY, FRED COMEGYS, THE WILMINGTON (DEL.) NEWS-JOURNAL

In the trenches (above), "Mean" Joe Deleski goes into a four-point stance. Only 16 players showed up for this annual affair, but for more than two hours they ran, huddled, threw — and got wet.

Re-living the good old days, Wayne Bradford plunges through for some yardage and recovers his own fumble (right).

GRAVY BOWL

Muddy alum (above) says it's worth it. A center (right) agrees; it's what Thanksgiving is all about, he says.

Spirit is willing but (this player determines) the body is less amenable than it was Way Back Then.

After the game, players get most of the mud off in a puddle before heading home for dinner. But they'll be back next year.

Above, Mike Woods, a speed skater from Wauwatosa, Wis., works out before a snow-filled grandstand in preparation for the Olympic trials. Right, wrestlers at the University of Wisconsin in Madison run stadium steps during an early autumn workout.

224

RICHARD D. SCHMIDT, THE SACRAMENTO (CALIF.) BEE

HELMUTH LOHMANN, ASSOCIATED PRESS

Above, competitors in a cross-country meet for California girls are a blur of action leaving the starting gate on a several-mile course. Right, Zamira Zaitseva from the Soviet Union rolls over the finish line to win silver medal in the women's 1,500 meter race at the World Track and Field championships in Helsinki, Finland. The Soviet girl fell as she headed for the finish line, then rolled herself to second place. Below, Evelyn Ashford, world's fastest woman, blazes to the relay finish line during National Sports Festival in Colorado Springs, Colo. Her relay team set a new American record in the event. Ashford later set a new world record in the 100 meter dash.

THIRD PLACE, NEWSPAPER SPORTS ACTION, PATRICK DOWNS, LOS ANGELES (CALIF.) TIMES

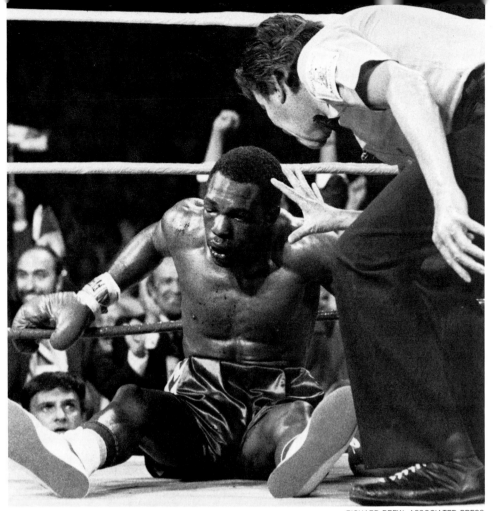

RICHARD DREW, ASSOCIATED PRESS

VICTOR, VANQUISHED: Right, Davey Moore takes a count of five in the seventh round of his WBA junior middleweight title bout with Roberto Duran. Below, Duran comes out of the ring to join with the crowd at Madison Square Garden in celebrating his third time as a champion.

AMY DAVIS, THE RECORD (HACKENSACK, N.J.)

Above, Mary Ellen Fletcher of Tucson, Ariz., pushes off on a downhill practice run in an attempt to earn a spot on the U.S. luge team for the 1984 Winter Olympics games in Sarajevo.

Below, Illinoisan Maris Anne Sternberg prepares to lift 415 pounds during a workout. The 195-pound 5-footer finished second in her class at the women's world power-lifting championships in Australia, later broke her own American records in four events.

High school twirlers make a sort of editorial comment about a Minnesota Vikings football game in Minneapolis.

HONORABLE MENTION, NEWSPAPER SPORTS FEATURE, REGENE RADNIECKI, MINNEAPOLIS (MINN.) STAR AND TRIBUNE

PAUL A. SCHMICK, THE WASHINGTON (D.C.) TIMES

Players for the Tampa Bay pro soccer team set their own priorities as Alan Green takes a penalty shot for Team America.

Above, Olympic hopeful Carl Lewis of the Santa Monica Track Club raises a cloud of sand and dust as he wins the long jump at UCLA Invitational with 28-1 mark. Left, a bull rider takes unwilling leave during Conejo Valley Days rodeo in Thousand Oaks, Calif.

In Wilkes-Barre, Pa., members of a VFW post team wait
for a rain squall to pass during a championship game.

Fifteen thousand people, participants in the San Francisco
Marathon, wind their way through Golden Gate Park on a
cold, foggy morning.

No. 41: an insider's view

By Joseph Costa

Journalism Lecturer
Ball State University

What do judges think about as they judge the Pictures of the Year competition? What are their impressions as they view some 20,000 images? I had judged more than one POY, both before and after the University of Missouri and National Press Photographers Association contests were merged.

I don't remember the thoughts I had in those earlier judgings, but having been asked to write about my impressions this time, I made notes while looking at the many images.

First, however, a few comments about the judging as a whole:

- Never have I seen a judging in which the students who handled the pictures were so efficient and well organized.

- Never have I seen such a well-balanced group of judges: two prize-winning staff photographers, the picture editor of Geo, a staff photographer of National Geographic, and the final member (myself), a photographer with more than 60 year's experience in photojournalism.

- I marveled at the intense interest of Cliff and Vi Edom, who attend the POY judging year after year. What a pleasure it was to see them! Also, Angus McDougall, now retired, and Bob Gilka, as adviser to the University of Missouri School of Journalism on POY, helped keep the judging moving smoothly. What a great service they render their profession!

- The sophistication of equipment used in the judging has vastly improved. I well remember sitting between Frank Scherschel of Life and Walter Yust, editor of Encyclopedia Britannica, that we held up "in" and "out" cards when screening a category. Here we press "in" and "out" buttons on small boxes to register our vote. Now none of the judges know how any of the others vote. The votes register on a master control box that lights green for "in" and red for "out"- but only after all the judges vote.

My impressions regarding the pictures:

- As the many portfolios passed before our eyes, I couldn't help thinking how the contestants would feel to see how quickly their best work had been disposed of. Because of the judges' expertise and the fact that some portfolios stood out head and shoulders above others, there could be no mistaking those that were outstanding.

- I recall that magazine photographers' entries used to be much stronger than those of newspaper photographers, but this year it was just the other way around.

- The real eye-stoppers seem divided into two groups: Those with great impact because of their content or subject matter, and those with unusual graphics or design elements. These are the things judges look for and instantly recognize.

- No doubt, far too much photojournalism is haphazard and sloppy. If photographers submit such work in competition, what kind of work must they be submitting to their editors?

- Why are there so many technically weak pictures entered? We all recognize when a weak picture has exceptionally good content. Indeed, some such entries are prize winners. But entries that are technically poor *and* badly printed have no place in any competition.

- NPPA's educational programs have greatly benefitted photojournalism. They will always be needed, since we never stop learning. Also, there will always be new, younger photographers coming along, as I once did some 64 years ago.

- Screening a category is easy enough, but it is much tougher to then decide on first, second and third place. It is awesome to realize how our decisions can affect an individual's career.

- When judging the pictorial category, I wondered where are the pictorialists and master printmakers such as A. Aubrey Bodine (now deceased) of The Baltimore (Md.) Sun. Will we ever again see a pictorialist with his talent?

- On viewing a picture story (see Page 156) about two lesbians, one of whom wanted to experience motherhood by having her own baby, it struck me how our culture has changed, in that people permit themselves to be pictured in the most private and intimate situations. Even in television, which has brought incredible changes to our society, we see the same thing occurring.

- When judging the picture story category, it was obvious that photographers do not seem to keep the picture editor in mind. They fail to produce "openers" facing into the page, or "closers" that face left rather than right to indicate a definite end. Some picture stories lack continuity and flow from picture to picture.

- Viewing all the entries, one gets the feeling that our world is not a nice place to live in. Many of the pictures and stories depict tragedy, misfortunes, and disaster; few, if any, are happy scenes.

Elisabeth Biondi, picture editor for Geo Magazine (one of the judges), put it this way: "On my way to Missouri I wondered what impression I would get of the past year by looking at the photo entries from 1983. I expected to see pass before my eyes photos of important events of the year, people who figured prominently and not-so-prominently, and pictures and/or stories about life's daily pleasures and pains — in other words, a review of the year.

"However, the emphasis in most of the strong stories I saw seemed to be sadness; the unhappiness and the misery of 1983.

"For example, the subject most frequently covered was people with missing limbs. These stories were poignant, their execution was excellent, and they were certainly valid. However, I could not help but think what a sad place the world reflected in these pictures seemed to be.

"Could it be that photojournalists have lost the ability to produce good stories about the pleasures of life; the simple, daily events that make up life? Or is it the reader who demands hard news all the time?

"Is only bad news, disaster, misery and sickness worthwhile news these days? If that is so, let's try to change it. We all know there is more to this world."

To which I ask, is it perhaps because in all of journalism, whether verbal or visual, we take the good things in life for granted? It must be recognized, however, that press photographers rarely choose their own assignments. They are told to cover this or that story — given their assignments by a superior — be it city editor, managing editor, chief photographer or whomever.

And isn't it true that the same thing can be said of all journalism, perhaps because stories about the

GREGG S. GOLDMAN

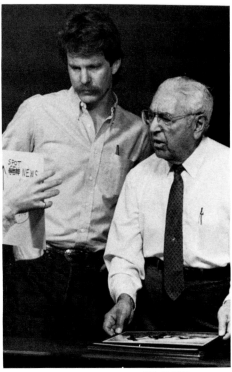

CAL OLSON

Judges of the 41st annual POY competition (clockwise from upper left): Jim Richardson, special projects photographer for The Denver (Colo.) Post; Elisabeth Biondi, picture editor of Geo Magazine; Pulitzer Prize-winner Jay Dickman of The Dallas (Texas) Times Herald; Joseph Costa, journalism lecturer at Ball State University, Bloomington, Ind.; Bruce Dale, National Geographic.

EDMUND LO

misfortunes of life seem to have the greatest psychological impact on readers? When people do good things — when a president, a governor or other public official does something right — it is expected of him. And so the happy stories are hardly ever mentioned — an unfortunate fact of life.

The most important impression I had was that despite the weaknesses and faults mentioned here, there are many fine photojournalists out there. They have great versatility and are able to capture the decisive moment, the human element, in any given situation, to make the event come alive. Thus photojournalism is in good hands for the forseeable future.

Finally, I felt good about the judging. I felt that as a judging panel, we had worked well together. After each category had been whittled down, the final eight or ten prints were

placed on racks. Not until then were we permitted to discuss the strengths and weaknesses of each print, picture story, or portfolio. That was when the real arguments among the judges began.

There was a great deal of give and take, with each judge holding firmly to his or her own opinions. But I also noticed something remarkable about how each argument was settled. In a letter I received after the judging, POY Director Ken Kobre tells what I noticed in his own words:

"What a great POY judging! Old-timers are still talking about how well the 41st contest came off. I can't believe how well all the judges worked together. Never have I seen five people maintain their own opinions, yet compromise gracefully through so many decisions."

That was how I felt.

The Winners

Newspaper division

SPOT NEWS:
First - Jorge Duran, Freelance for United Press International, "Flee gas balloon explosion"
Second - Anthony Suau, The Denver (Colo.) Post, "Highway standoff"
Third - Tom Van Dyke, San Jose (Calif.) Mercury News, "Fighting the flood"
Honorable mention: Jimi Lott, Spokane (Wash.) Review and Chronicle, "The big one"
Honorable mention: Alberto Garcia, Associated Press, "Death in the streets"
Honorable mention: Bill Foley, Associated Press, "Easy does it"

GENERAL NEWS:
First - Anthony Suau, The Denver (Colo.) Post, "Grief"
Second - Tom Salyer, United Press International, "Well-armed swimmers"
Third - Pat Tehan, Santa Ana (Calif.) Register, "Protester"
Honorable mention - David I. Andersen, The Plain Dealer (Cleveland, Ohio) "Mishleen"
Honorable mention: Jim Damaske, Clearwater (Fla.) Sun, "Legal briefs"

FEATURE PICTURE:
First - Paul Miller, Freelance for the Hartford (Conn.) Courant, "Balancing act"
Second - Steve Ringman, San Francisco (Calif.) Chronicle, "Assaulted by the wind"
Third - Barbara Montgomery, The Courier Journal, Louisville (Ky.) Times, "Senior citizens' dance"
Honorable mention - Joe Abell, San Angelo (Texas) Standard-Times, "Symphonic shadows"
Honorable mention - Rick T. Wilking, United Press International, "Getting in a quick nine"

Honorable mention - Michael Bryant, San Jose (Calif.) Mercury News, "Cutting through the red tape"

SPORTS ACTION:
First - Jimi Lott, Spokane (Wash.) Review and Chronicle, "Over easy"
Second - Michael Delaney, The Miami (Fla.) News "Arrugumphhh!"
Third - Patrick Downs, Los Angeles (Calif.) Times, "Evelyn at speed"
Honorable mention - Joe Patronite, The Arizona Daily Star (Tucson), "Bull and matador"
Honorable mention - Phil Skinner, News and Sun-Sentinel, (Fort Lauderdale, Fla.), "Free-for-all at the goal"
Honorable mention - Raymond Gehman, The Virginian Pilot/Ledger Star, "Rebound at the rim"

SPORTS FEATURE:
First - Paul F. Moseley, Fort Worth (Texas) Star-Telegram, "The champ doesn't have to walk"
Second - William Meyer, Newspapers, Inc. (Milwaukee, Wis.), "Solitary skater"
Third - Michael Rondou, The Hartford (Conn.) Courant, "Boston says good-bye"
Honorable mention - Regene Radniecki, Minneapolis (Minn.) Star-Tribune, "End of an exciting game"
Honorable mention - Ken Bizzigotti, Wilkes-Barre (Pa.) Times-Leader, "Rained out"
Honorable mention - Chris Walker, Chicago (Ill.) Tribune, "Catch of the day"

PORTRAIT PERSONALITY:
First - Jimi Lott, Spokane (Wash.) Review and Chronicle, "Fuzzy friend"
Second - Victoria Yokota, The Washington (D.C.) Times, "The weight of the world"

hird - Jim Gensheimer, The Louisville (Ky.) Courier-Journal, "Tears for Jesus"
onorable mention - Carol Guzy, The Miami (Fla.) Herald, "Sam and Marie"

ICTORIAL:
rst - Bern Ketchum, Topeka (Kan.) Capital-Journal, "Spark of life"
econd - Gary Gunderson, The Litchfield County Times (New Milford, Conn.), "White on white on white"
hird - Tom Burton, The Orlando (Fla.) Sentinel, "A layup and two points"
onorable mention - Dru Nadler, The Advocate (Stamford, Conn.), "Pig"
onorable mention - Don Petersen, Roanoke (Va.) Times and World News, "Stacked up"

DITORIAL ILLUSTRATION:
irst - Eugene Louie, San Jose (Calif.) Mercury News, "Up from alcoholism"
econd - Jim Mendenhall, San Jose (Calif.) Mercury News, "Build your own house"
hird - Michael S. Wirtz, Dallas (Texas) Times Herald, "Execution"
onorable mention - William Snyder, The Dallas (Texas) Morning News, " . . . but it's good for you"
onorable mention - Chuck Zoeller, Wilkes-Barre (Pa.) Times-Leader, "Soft lens/hard wear"

ASHION ILLUSTRATION:
irst - Tony Berardi, Chicago (Ill.) Tribune, "Woman in chains"
econd - Marice Carolyn Cohn, The Miami (Fla.) Herald, "Fall hues"
hird - Nick Kelsh, The Philadelphia (Pa.) Inquirer, "Fur"
onorable mention - John R. Van Beekum, Houston (Texas) Chronicle, "Chanel leaps into fashion"
onorable mention - Tom A. Walker, Calgary (Sask.) Herald, "Venetian sunglasses"

OOD ILLUSTRATION:
irst - Michael Bryant, San Jose (Calif.) Mercury News, "Stuffed potatoes"
econd (tie) - Alan Berner, The Seattle (Wash.) Times, "Washington state cheese snack"
econd (tie) - Marna Clarke, Freelance for The Hartford (Conn.) Courant, "Hot peppers"

Third - Don Kohlbauer, The San Diego (Calif.) Union-Tribune, "Artichoke"
Honorable mention - Michael Bryant, San Jose (Calif.) Mercury News, "American classics"
Honorable mention - G. Andrew Boyd, The Times Picayune (New Orleans, La.), "Goldfish martini"

NEWS PICTURE STORY:
First - Anthony Suau, The Denver (Colo.) Post, "Rush hour confrontation"
Second - David Peterson, The Des Moines (Iowa) Register, "A good soldier comes home"
Third - Jimi Lott, Spokane (Wash.) Review and Chronicle, "Killer quake"
Honorable mention - John Kaplan, The Spokane (Wash.) Spokesman-Review, "Tribute"
Honorable mention - Anthony Suau, The Denver (Colo.) Post, "Ethiopia: land of desperation"

FEATURE PICTURE STORY:
First - Steve Ringman, San Francisco (Calif.) Chronicle, "Fighting together against AIDs"
Second - Michael Bryant, San Jose (Calif.) Mercury News, "Donny Valone comes home"
Third - Jimi Lott, Spokane (Wash.) Review and Chronicle, "The Basque"
Honorable mention - Rick Rickman, Santa Ana (Calif.) Register, "The partnership"

SPORTS PICTURE STORY:
First - Raymond Gehman, The Virginian Pilot/Ledger Star (Norfolk, Va.), "Wrestling with a dream"
Second - Dave LaBelle, Ogden (Utah) Standard Examiner, "One dream ends, another begins"
Third - Fred Comegys, The News-Journal Co. (Wilmington, Del.), "The annual turkey bowl"
Honorable mention - Anthony Suau, The Denver (Colo.) Post, "Blood, sweat and jeers"

SELF-PRODUCED PUBLISHED PICTURE STORY — BROADSHEET
First - Bill Greene, Quincy (Mass.) Patriot Ledger, "Between heaven and earth"

SELF-PRODUCED PUBLISHED PICTURE STORY — MULTI-PAGE, TABLOID:
First - Richard Marshall, The Ithaca (N.Y.) Journal, "The over-the-hill gang"

Magazine division

NEWS/DOCUMENTARY:
irst - Mustafa Bozdemir, Hurriyet for Life, "After the quake, a Turkish mother's anguish"
econd - Jose Azel, Contact Press Images for Life, "A tense papal visit to Central America"
hird - Jan Morvan, Sipa Press/Black Star for Life, "Suffer the little children"
onorable mention - Alfred Yaghodzadeh, Sygma for Newsweek, "Tripoli: home, sweet home"
onorable mention - Jan Morvan, Sipa Press/Black Star for Life, "Bloody Sunday"

FEATURE:
irst - James Nachtwey, Black Star for Time, "Monument to the revolution"

Second - Michael Melford, Wheeler Pictures for GEO, "Japanese drummers"
Third - Annie Griffiths, National Geographic, "The Citadel"
Honorable mention - James L. Amos, National Geographic, "Scala Sancta"
Honorable mention - Gerald Martineau, Washington (D.C.) Post for Life, "Just one more"

SPORTS:
First - Alain Guillou, Visions for Life, "Off they go, into the wild bleu yonder"
Second - Joel Baldwin, Freelance for GEO, "Coaching accident"
Third - George Tiedemann, Sports Illustrated (contract), untitled

Magazine Winners (cont'd.)

Honorable mention - George Tiedemann, Sports Illustrated (contract), untitled

Honorable mention - John Dominis, Wheeler Pictures for Life, "High divers"

PORTRAIT PERSONALITY:
First - Michael O'Neill, Freelance for Life, "Larry King"
Second - Michael O'Neill, Freelance for Life, "The bodies beneath the pads"
Third - William Coupon, Freelance for GEO, "Arthur C. Clarke"
Honorable mention - David Burnett, Contact Press Images for New York Times Magazine, "John Glenn"
Honorable mention - James Nachtwey, Black Star for Time, "Weary of war"

PICTORIAL:
First - Ferdinando Scianna, Magnum for Life, "Nature's rage"
Second - Henry Groskinsky, Freelance for Life, "A birthday blast for a grand old span"
Third - Richard W. Brown, Blair & Ketchum's Country Journal, "Plowing scene"
Honorable mention - James L. Standfield, National Geographic, "Holy grottoes of Cappadocia"

SCIENCE/NATURAL HISTORY:
First - Sam Walton, United Press International for Life, "Nature's rage"
Second - Alexander Tsiaras, Freelance for Life, "Treating the unborn patient"
Third - Jeff Simons, Freelance for Life, "Whales vs. nets"
Honorable mention - Kim Steele, Freelance for Life, "Harvesting the winds"

PUBLISHED PICTURE STORY:
First - Mary Ellen Mark, Archive for Life, "Streets of the lost"
Second - Michael O'Neill, Freelance for GEO, "Taiwan art"
Third - Tomas Sennet, Freelance for GEO, "Faulkner"
Honorable mention - Michael K. Nichols, Magnum for GEO, "Rope"

SELF-EDITED PICTURE STORY:
First - James Nachtwey, Black Star for Time, "Battle for Souk Al Garb"
Second - James L. Stanfield, National Geographic, "Village of the past"
Third - Ethan Hoffman, Freelance for Life, "Corporate boot camp in Japan"
Honorable mention - David Doubilet, National Geographic, "Dolphin slaughter in Japan"

Editing awards

BEST USE OF PHOTOGRAPHS BY A NEWSPAPER:
Jackson Hole (Wyo.) News

NEWSPAPER PICTURE EDITOR AWARD:
David Fitzsimmons, The Virginian Pilot/Ledger Star (Norfolk, Va.)

NEWSPAPER-MAGAZINE PICTURE EDITOR AWARD:
James Noel Smith, Westward (Dallas Times Herald)

BEST USE OF PHOTOGRAPHS BY A MAGAZINE:
International Wildlife Magazine

MAGAZINE PICTURE EDITOR AWARD:
Bruce A. McElfresh, National Geographic

NEWSPAPER PICTURE EDITOR: DAVID FITZSIMMONS, THE VIRGINIAN PILOT/LEDGER STAR (NORFOLK, VA.)

BEST USE OF PHOTOGRAPHS BY A NEWSPAPER:
JACKSON HOLE (WYO.) NEWS

MAGAZINE PICTURE EDITOR AWARD:
BRUCE A. McELFRESH, NATIONAL GEOGRAPHIC

BEST USE OF PHOTOGRAPHS BY A MAGAZINE:
INTERNATIONAL WILDLIFE MAGAZINE

NEWSPAPER-MAGAZINE PICTURE EDITOR AWARD:
JAMES NOEL SMITH, WESTWARD (DALLAS TIMES HERALD)

Index to photographers

They're everywhere,
they're everywhere

JEFF HORNER, WALLA WALLA (WASH.) UNION-BULLETIN

DAVID SPRAGUE, THE DAILY TEXAN (AUSTI

JAMES COLBURN, PHOTOREPORTERS FOR USA TODAY

GEORGE LANGE, AMERICAN PHOTOGRAPHE

BRUCE GILBERT, MIAMI (FLA.) HERALD

DAVID HUME KENNERLY, TIM